SHAKESPEARE

JULIUS CAESAR IN EVERYDAY ENGLISH

COLES EDITORIAL BOARD

Bound to stay open

Publisher's Note

Otabind (Ota-bind). This book has been bound using the patented Otabind process. You can open this book at any page, gently run your finger down the spine, and the pages will lie flat.

ABOUT COLES NOTES

COLES NOTES have been an indispensible aid to students on five continents since 1948.

COLES NOTES are available for a wide range of individual literary works. Clear, concise explanations and insights are provided along with interesting interpretations and evaluations.

Proper use of COLES NOTES will allow the student to pay greater attention to lectures and spend less time taking notes. This will result in a broader understanding of the work being studied and will free the student for increased participation in discussions.

COLES NOTES are an invaluable aid for review and exam preparation as well as an invitation to explore different interpretive paths.

COLES NOTES are written by experts in their fields. It should be noted that any literary judgement expressed herein is just that – the judgement of one school of thought. Interpretations that diverge from, or totally disagree with any criticism may be equally valid.

COLES NOTES are designed to supplement the text and are not intended as a substitute for reading the text itself. Use of the NOTES will serve not only to clarify the work being studied, but should enhance the readers enjoyment of the topic.

ISBN 0-7740-2994-3

© COPYRIGHT 2005 AND PUBLISHED BY
COLES PUBLISHING COMPANY
TORONTO - CANADA
PRINTED IN CANADA

Manufactured by Webcom Limited
Cover finish: Webcom's Exclusive **DURACOAT**

CHARACTERS IN THE PLAY

Julius Caesar
Octavius Caesar
Mark Antony
M. Aemilius Lepidus } Triumvirs after the death of Julius Caesar.

Cicero
Publius
Popilius Lena } Senators.

Marcus Brutus
Cassius
Casca
Trebonius
Ligarius
Decius Brutus
Metellus Cimber
Cinna } Conspirators against Julius Caesar.

Flavius and Marullus: Tribunes.
Artemidorus: A sophist.
Soothsayer
Cinna: A poet.
Another Poet

Lucilius
Titinius
Messala
Young Cato
Volumnius } Friends of Brutus and Cassius.

Varro
Clitus
Claudius
Strato
Lucilius
Dardanius } Servants of Brutus.

Pindarus: Servant of Cassius.
Calphurnia: Caesar's wife.
Portia: Brutus' wife.
The ghost of Caesar
Senators, Citizens, Guards and Attendants.

[Setting: Rome, near Sardis and near Philippi.]

ACT I • SCENE 1

[Rome, a street.]
[Enter Flavius, Marullus and certain commoners.]

Flavius: Now then, you lazy fellows, go home and get on with your work. You know very well that today is not a holiday. You certainly ought to be aware that, as you are working men, it is illegal for you to be in the streets without wearing the badge denoting your trade. Here, what is your trade?

First Commoner: Mine? Oh, I'm a carpenter, your honor.

Marullus: Why are you not wearing your leather apron then, or carrying your rule? How is it that you are dressed in your best clothes? And you, also, what is your occupation?

Second Commoner: Well really, sir, when compared with skilled artisans, I should be considered but a clumsy workman.

Marullus: Come now, don't evade my question. What is your trade?

Second Commoner: Well, sir, it is one that I have no reason to be ashamed of, for I repair and restore the soles of others.

Marullus: You good-for-nothing rascal, tell me immediately what your occupation is.

Second Commoner: Oh come, sir, you need not be so put out, although I can easily restore you, even if you be.

Marullus: You impudent rascal, what are you talking about? What do you mean by restoring me?

Second Commoner: Well, sir, I mean that I can patch you up again.

Flavius: Do you mean to say that you are a cobbler?

Second Commoner: Yes, sir, it is with the awl that I earn my living. My business is with awl, although I never interfere with other people's business. I am a repairer of old boots, and when they are nearly worn out, I make them as good as new again. I can assure you that I have repaired the shoes of the best men in the state.

Flavius: Well, how is it that you are not at work today? Why are you encouraging these men to roam the streets, instead of attending to your business?

Second Commoner: Well, to tell the truth, sir, I am attending to my business in doing so, for if they wear their boots out, I shall get the job of repairing them. But we are really out to

1

see Caesar, and to share in the festivities accompanying his triumph.

Marullus: What cause is there for such festivities? What new country has he subdued? What prisoners are they that he is bringing to Rome to enhance his triumph by being dragged in chains behind his chariot? You stupid fellows, you idiots, you cruel, hard-hearted Romans, have you forgotten Pompey? Why, in the past, whenever you heard that Pompey was to pass along the streets of Rome, you used to throng every point of vantage along the route, no matter how difficult of access, in your eagerness merely to catch sight of him. You have thought it no hardship even to have to sit there with your children in your arms the whole day long, if there was any chance of seeing him at all. As soon as you caught sight of his chariot, your loud and ringing cheers were such that they were echoed again and again from the hollow banks of the Tiber. Yet, now, dressing yourselves in your best and choosing this day for a holiday, you come out to do honor to the person who makes a triumph because he has defeated the sons of Pompey. Be off! Hasten back to your homes and, bowing yourselves in penitence before the gods, pray that you may be spared the just punishment that should reward such ingratitude.

Flavius: Yes! Go home, my friends, and, as a penance, call together your fellow workmen. Conduct them to the banks of the river and shed tears of repentance until the river, although it may be at its lowest, shall be so swelled by them that it shall reach to the highest banks.

[Exit all the commoners.]

It is evident that our words have impressed them and that they perceive their ingratitude, for see, they depart without a word. You go toward the Capitol in that direction, and I will go in this. If you see any decorations on the statues, remove them.

Marullus: But will it be allowed? Remember that the Lupercalia is held today.

Flavius: That makes no difference. Do not permit Caesar's trophies to adorn the statues. I will do what I can to send the common people home. You do the same wherever you see them congregated together. These little checks upon Caesar's ambition will warn him not to aspire too high.

Otherwise he will so get the upper hand that our very liberties will be threatened.

[Exit.]

ACT I • SCENE 2

[A public place.]

[Flourish of trumpets. Enter Caesar, Antony, Calphurnia, Portia, Decius, Cicero, Brutus, Cassius and Casca; a great crowd following, among them a soothsayer.]

Caesar: Calphurnia!

Casca: Silence! Caesar is speaking.

Caesar: Calphurnia!

Calphurnia: Yes, my lord?

Caesar: When Antony commences to run, I wish you to place yourself immediately in his path. Antony!

Antony: Yes, my lord?

Caesar: Antony, I wish you to touch Calphurnia during your running, as it is believed by our wise men that women afflicted with barrenness become fruitful if so touched by the runner.

Antony: I will not forget. It is sufficient for me to know that it is Caesar's will.

Caesar: Proceed then, and be careful that all the rites are performed correctly, down to the smallest details.

[Flourish of trumpets.]

Soothsayer: Caesar!

Caesar: Who is calling me?

Casca: Let no one make any sound. Silence!

Caesar: Who called my name from amid the crowd? I heard a voice distinctly, above all the sounds of the trumpets, calling my name. Whoever he be, let him now speak, for I am listening.

Soothsayer: The 15th of March will prove dangerous to you.

Caesar: Who is it speaking?

Brutus: A prophet says that the 15th of March will be full of danger for you.

Caesar: Bring him here, and let him confront me.

Cassius: Here, come forward. Make your way out of the crowd. Caesar asks for you.

Caesar: Now then, what information is this that you are anxious to give me? Tell me again.

Soothsayer: The 15th of March will prove dangerous to you.

Caesar: Nonsense! We will not listen to him. Let us go.

[Exit all but Cassius and Brutus.]

Cassius: Are you going to witness the running?

Brutus: No, I am not.

Cassius: Oh, come now, do.

Brutus: No, I am not sportively inclined. My temperament is not of so lively a character as that of Antony. Still, I have no wish to prevent you from going. I will, therefore, bid you farewell.

Cassius: Look here, Brutus, I have been watching you rather closely lately, and your looks nowadays are not so full of that amiability and evident affection for me as they used to be. You treat me, who bear you so much regard, with an undeserved harshness and coldness of manner.

Brutus: You are mistaken, Cassius. If at times I have not met you with the same affectionate looks as in former days, it is because I am constantly endeavoring not to appear worried or troubled in the presence of others. I am, and have been for some time, disturbed by conflicting emotions and with thoughts concerning private matters, and these perhaps make my manner toward others appear less courteous than usual. But I should not like my friends to be worried on this account — and you may be assured that I include you among them, Cassius — or to attribute my change of manner to any other cause than that, distracted by my troubles, I have sometimes forgotten to show those outward courtesies due to my fellow men.

Cassius: In that case, Brutus, I see I was wrong about the feeling by which you were influenced. Through this mistake of mine, I have been led to keep to myself many thoughts and ideas of sufficient worth and importance to be communicated to others. Now, tell me, Brutus, is it possible for you to see your own countenance?

Brutus: Certainly not, Cassius. It is impossible for the eye to see itself: all it can do is to see its image reflected from other objects.

Cassius: You are quite right, and there are a great many people, Brutus, who regret that there are no mirrors capable of reflecting the image of your worthiness, which is at present concealed from you, or mirrors that could enable you to see yourself as you really are. It has come to my knowledge that many people, including those held in the highest esteem in Rome — of course, I do not include the godlike Caesar — who, while they have been discussing Brutus and bemoaning the tyranny and oppression of the present time, have expressed the wish that Brutus could see himself as they see him.

Brutus: Into what perilous schemes are you seeking to persuade me, Cassius, that you should thus pretend to find in me virtues and moral qualities that are non-existent?

Cassius: Listen to me, Brutus. As you are already aware, it is impossible for you to see yourself well, except by the aid of some reflecting medium. I will, therefore, act as your mirror and reveal to you, without any exaggeration, those qualities that you possess, but of which you are at present ignorant. I beg you also, Brutus, not to be so suspicious of me. If I were prone to joking or were in the habit of swearing friendship and regard for every newcomer who professed the same for me, and had thus made such protestations worthless, or if it were a matter of common knowledge that I flattered men to their faces and spoke evil of them behind their backs or that I made protestations of friendship to every companion, then you could regard me as a man who was not to be trusted.

[Flourish of trumpets and shout.]

Brutus: What are all the people shouting for? I am afraid they intend to offer Caesar the crown.

Cassius: You say that you are afraid of it? Then I presume you would rather such a thing did not happen.

Brutus: I certainly would, Cassius, although, personally, I have a sincere regard for him. But what reason have you for detaining me? You evidently have something to tell me. If the matter be one tending to the public welfare, I care not whether it lead to honor or death. I shall equally regard either and will as soon meet death as attain honor, for, I can assure you, the reputation of being an honorable man is more to me than even life itself.

Cassius: I am as well aware of the nobleness of your nature as I am of your personal appearance. Still, what I have to talk about concerns honor most closely.

I do not know what your thoughts may be about this life,

5

nor what those of others may be, but, as for myself, I would just as soon be dead as live in fear of one who, like myself, is only mortal. My birth was as noble as that of Caesar, and so was yours. We have both been equally well brought up, and neither of us is one bit inferior to him in bodily endurance. Why, I remember, one very cold and windy day, when the swollen Tiber was angrily dashing its waves against its restraining banks, Caesar accosted me in this way: "Are you brave enough, Cassius, to jump into this rushing torrent and swim to that point there?" I did not hesitate a moment, but asking him to do the same, I immediately jumped in just as I was, with all my clothes on, and he followed me.

The force of the current was so great that we had to use all our strength and energy to keep ourselves from being swept away. Before we reached the point agreed upon, Caesar's strength failed him and he cried, "Lend me your aid, Cassius, or I shall be drowned." I went to his assistance and, even as our distinguished forefather, Aeneas, saved his aged father, Anchises, from the burning city of Troy by carrying him away on his shoulders, so did I hold up the exhausted Caesar and save him from being drowned in the Tiber. And now he is regarded as divine, Cassius being considered a mere nobody who is expected to bow with the utmost reverence if Caesar condescends enough to acknowledge him with a careless nod.

While in Spain he was stricken with fever, and I noticed that he was seized with the same tremblings as other men, although he is now considered divine. His lips became white and those eyes, whose mere glance now strikes terror into the whole world, lost their brightness. Groans were heard issuing from his lips. Yes! That same voice that so boastfully ordered the Roman scribes to keep a record of all his acts and words cried, "Fetch me something to drink, Titinius," as pitifully as any sick maiden. I am surprised that so weak a man should obtain so great an advantage over all others as to thus carry off the prize.

[Shout. Flourish of trumpets.]

Brutus: The people are cheering again. From these acclamations, it is evident they are conferring further honors upon Caesar.

Cassius: My dear fellow, his ambition knows no bounds. We insignificant creatures may be said to walk beneath his legs, as beneath those of a Colossus, and all that we dare to do is to timidly look around for graves in which we may hide our dishonor. At one time or another, every man has control over his own destiny. There is no need to blame the stars that may have been in the ascendant at our birth, for it is our own fault if we remain contented with an inferior position. Compare the names of Brutus and Caesar. What is there about the name of Caesar, that it should be on the lips of all, while yours is scarcely mentioned? If they are written down, your name looks as well as his. If you pronounce them, yours sounds every bit as good. They both contain the same number of letters and, if they were used as spells, it would be as easy to invoke a spirit with yours as with his.

By whatever means is Caesar thus enabled to surpass all others in greatness? Such things put thee to shame, O age! And thou, O Rome, hast surely lost thy race of illustrious men. Never since the deluge has a single age passed by that was not made famous by a large number of great men. Never before could anyone say, when speaking about Rome, that there was only one man of distinction within her extensive bounds. At the present time, however, this is not the case, and, as there appears to be but one person in the whole of Rome, there certainly ought to be no crowding or jostling. Why, we have been told by our parents that a Brutus once existed who would as soon have allowed Satan himself to hold supreme power in Rome as to allow a king to do so.

Brutus: I do not in any way doubt the sincerity of your regard for me, and I think I can guess what you would have me do. I will tell you later the result of my deliberations, both on this subject and on the condition of the state at the present time. Meanwhile, I would in all friendship beg you not to press me further. I will give careful thought to those matters upon which you have spoken, and will patiently listen to whatever proposals you may have to bring forward, and will also appoint a suitable date for the discussion of these important matters.

In the meantime, my friend, I may tell you this; that I

would much prefer to live in a village than call myself a Roman citizen if I am compelled to submit to such tyranny and oppression as seem likely to come upon us before long.

Cassius: It pleases me to find that my poor eloquence has been able to evoke even these slight signs of warmth from such a one as Brutus.

Brutus: The sports are over, and Caesar is coming back.

Cassius: While the people are going by, attract Casca's attention, and you will then hear from him everything that has happened today worth hearing, although he will relate it in his own morose, caustic way.

[Re-enter Caesar and his followers.]

Brutus: I will follow your suggestion. Do you notice, Cassius, that flush of anger on Caesar's face? The others, too, look as if they had been rebuked by their master. See how pale Calphurnia is! Cicero, too, with his red, ferret like eyes, is looking as he often looks in the senate house when thwarted by his fellow legislators.

Cassius: We shall hear all about it from Casca.

Caesar: Antony!

Antony: Yes, Caesar?

Caesar: See that the men who usually surround me are stout, that their hair is smoothly combed and that they are inclined to be wakeful at night. Cassius, there, looks thin and almost starved, evidently grown thin with too much thinking. There is danger to be feared from such men.

Antony: You need not be afraid of him, Caesar. No danger is to be feared from him, for he is of gentle birth and is well disposed.

Caesar: I would rather he were not so thin, although I am not afraid of him. Still, if I knew what fear was, there is no man whom I should so much fear as that thin fellow, Cassius. He is evidently given to study. He notices everything, and his mental vision would be such as would pierce beneath the surface of men's actions in order to discover their motives. He is different from you, Antony, for he does not care for plays. Nor is he fond of music. He does not often smile, and, even when he does, it is in a derisive manner, as if he despised himself for being so weak as to give way to so childish an emotion. Men of his disposition are never contented as long as there remains another man holding a better position. On this account, one should beware of such men. Remember, I am merely mentioning what might be feared. I do not mean to say that I am afraid, for Caesar knows not fear. Come to the other side, for I am somewhat deaf in my left ear, and let me hear your real opinion of Cassius.

[Exit Caesar and all his followers but Casca.]

Casca: You tried to attract my attention just now. Did you wish to say anything to me?

Brutus: Yes, Casca. We would like to hear an account of today's proceedings and why Caesar appears so troubled and annoyed.

Casca: Were you not present?

Brutus: If I had been, it would not have been necessary for me to ask you about it.

Casca: Oh, the people wanted him to take the crown, but he refused it, motioning it away, like this. Then, all the people cheered him.

Brutus: Why did they cheer him the second time?

Casca: Oh, for the same reason.

Cassius: But I heard them cheering three times. Why did they cheer the third time?

Casca: Still for the same reason.

Brutus: Why, did they offer him the crown three times?

Casca: Yes, they did, and he motioned it away three times, each time more gently than before, and the people cheered loudly at each refusal.

Cassius: By whom was the crown thus offered to him?

Casca: Oh, by Antony.

Brutus: Well, my good Casca, describe the way in which it was all done.

Casca: That I could not possibly do. I really did not notice it very closely, for the whole thing was absurd. I certainly saw Mark Antony offer Caesar a crown, or, rather, a wreath and, as I said before, he motioned it away, although, in my opinion, he would rather have accepted it. It was again offered to him, and he again refused it, but I am sure he did so with great reluctance. It was offered a third time, and for the third time he refused it. Each time he put it aside, the mob cheered and clapped their hands, tossed their grimy caps into the air and shouted so much that Caesar was nearly suffocated by the foul air issuing from their lips. He fell down in a faint, and I myself was afraid to open my mouth to laugh in fear that I should be similarly affected.

Cassius: Wait a bit. Do you mean to say that Caesar fainted?

Casca: Yes, he fell prostrate in the forum. He was unable to speak, and foam issued from his lips.

Brutus: It is quite possible, for he is subject to epileptic fits.

Cassius: For my part, instead of Caesar, I think it is you and I and good Casca here who are so afflicted, that we are in the habit of falling down and prostrating ourselves.

Casca: I do not understand you. I am certain, however, that Caesar fell. And I am also certain that he was applauded by those of the mob who were pleased at his action, and hissed by those who were not, just as the actors are applauded and hissed in the theater. If he were not, then never believe me again.

Brutus: What did he say when he recovered?

Casca: Well, just before he fainted, seeing that the rabble was pleased at his refusal of the crown, he tore his shirt open and gave them permission to take his life if they wished to do so. If I had been one of them, or even a man of action, you may be sure I would have quickly done so. Well, he then fainted. As soon as he recovered he begged that if he had displeased them in any way, either by word or deed, they would attribute it to his state of health. Several women standing near me cried out "Poor fellow" and professed themselves quite willing to pardon him anything. It is useless, however, to take any notice of these, for they would have said the same even if their own mother had been done to death by him.

Brutus: And did he then come away with that grave look upon his face?

Casca: Yes.

Cassius: Was any speech made by Cicero?

Casca: Yes, he said something in Greek.

Cassius: What did he say?

Casca: I do not know, for I could not understand him, but those who did exchanged smiles with one another, and I saw them shaking their heads. As far as I am concerned, his speech was unintelligible. There is, however, something else to tell. Marullus and Flavius have been arrested for removing the decorations from Caesar's statues. Good-bye. There were other absurd doings, but I have forgotten them.

Cassius: Will you come home with me to supper, Casca?

Casca: No, thank you, I have an engagement this evening.

Cassius: Well, will you come to dinner tomorrow?

Casca: Yes, if all is well; that is, provided you do not change your mind and that the dinner is a good one.

Cassius: Very well, we will consider that settled.

Casca: All right. Good-bye, both of you.

[Exit.]

Brutus: How dull and unintelligent he seems to have become! Why, in his school days, he appeared quite sharp.

Cassius: You will find him so still, if he has anything brave or great to do, although he may now affect this sluggish temperament. This bluntness of manner merely gives an additional zest to his caustic wit and makes it more pleasing to those who listen to him.

Brutus: You are quite right. I must go now, however. If you wish to resume our conversation, I will either come to your house tomorrow or, if you care to come to mine, I will make a point of being at home.

Cassius: Very well, I will come to yours. In the meantime, ponder over the present state of affairs.

[Exit Brutus.]

Well, you are certainly a most honorable man, Brutus. Still, it is plain enough that your nature, noble as it is, may be easily influenced in another direction. It is well, therefore, that honorable natures should make a point of associating only with those of similar character. After all, there are very few so strong-minded that it is impossible to lead them astray. Caesar certainly has a grudge against me, but he has none against Brutus. Now, if I could change places with Brutus, I would not allow myself to be so influenced by him as he is by me. This evening, I will throw some letters into the windows of his room, all in different handwritings, as if written by different people, and all of which shall discuss the high estimation in which Brutus is held by his fellow citizens. In them all, I will darkly hint at Caesar's ambition. After that, Caesar had better see that his present position is impregnable, for either he must fall or we shall have to put up with still greater tyranny and oppression.

ACT I • SCENE 3

[A street.]

[Thunder and lightning. Enter from opposite sides, Casca, with his sword drawn, and Cicero.]

Cicero: Good evening, Casca. Did you accompany Caesar back from the course? Why, what has made you so out of breath? What has scared you?

Casca: Does it not frighten you, when all the laws of nature seem thus to be suspended? I have certainly witnessed terrible storms, Cicero, ones in which the strongest oaks have been felled by the violence of the wind, and have seen the storm-tossed waves of the ocean rising mountains high. But never before have I witnessed such a storm as I have this evening. Why, the clouds have actually been raining fire. The gods must either be at war between themselves, or their intention must be to destroy the earth as a punishment for men's unfaithfulness.

Cicero: Why, what more marvellous things have you beheld?

Casca: I saw an ordinary slave — one well-known to you by the way — holding up his left hand, which appeared to be on fire, and which emitted as much light as 20 torches put together. He did not, however, appear to suffer any inconvenience, and his hand was not even scorched by the fire. Then, close to the senate house, I encountered a lion — I've kept my sword unsheathed since then. It looked fiercely at me but passed on, leaving me unmolested. I also met a large number of women, pale with terror, all huddled together, who insisted that they had seen men clothed in flames walking along the streets and highways. Yesterday, too, an owl was heard, in broad daylight, uttering its cries in the forum. When so many portents are observed, so nearly together and at the same time, it is useless for people to say to me, "oh, these things can easily be accounted for, they proceed from perfectly natural causes," for, in my opinion, they forbode disaster to the country where they occur.

Cicero: These are certainly most unaccountable times. It is quite possible that people, interpreting these phenomena in their own way, may find their conclusions totally at variance with the truth. Is Caesar coming to the senate house tomorrow?

Casca: Yes, he told Antony to tell you that he intended to be present.

Cicero: Well, good night, Casca. This is certainly not a night to be out-of-doors.

Casca: Good-bye, Cicero.

[Exit Cicero.]
[Enter Cassius.]

Cassius: Ah! Who is that?

Casca: A citizen of Rome.

Cassius: Ah! That is Casca's voice, I know.

Casca: You certainly have a keen ear. What is your opinion of this night?

Cassius: Those who have clear consciences need have no fear of it.

Casca: Have the heavens ever before been known to be so threatening?

Cassius: Has such wickedness ever before been known in the world as at the present time? As far, however, as I myself am concerned, I have been walking up and down the streets and have not tried in any way to avoid the dangers of the night. I have undone my coat, Casca, as you can see, and have not hesitated to expose my breast to the thunderbolt, and have even stood directly in the way of the lightning as it flashed across the sky.

Casca: But what reason had you for so exposing yourself? When such terrible messengers are sent by the almighty gods to thus warn us, we ought to conduct ourselves in reverent fear and trembling.

Cassius: You are evidently slow of understanding, Casca, and you are either devoid of that intelligence that every Roman should possess or, if you have it, you do not exercise it. You show all the signs of fear and appear lost in amazement at these strange manifestations. Yet, if you only gave a little thought to the real reason for all these things — why such fire descends, why these disembodied spirits are seen gliding about the streets, why birds and animals act contrary to their natural dispositions, why the aged act like children while children show wisdom beyond their years and why all these show such deviations from the ordinary laws that

13

regulate their being — you will easily see that the gods have caused these deviations to inspire men with awe and serve as portents of some coming disaster. I think, Cassius, I could tell you the name of a man who much resembles this terrible night, a man who endeavors by his acts to inspire men with fear, who is proud, haughty and overbearing even in the senate house, a man who, after all, has done no more than you or I, but who has attained such great power and influence that he is to be feared as much as these unfamiliar phenomena.

Casca: I presume you are alluding to Caesar, are you not?

Cassius: I will not mention names, for, although the people of Rome still resemble their forefathers in possessing muscles and limbs, their ready submission to oppression shows, alas, that they have not inherited that independent spirit that belonged to their ancestors. They have become weak and effeminate.

Casca: You are not far wrong. It is rumored that the senate intend to make Caesar king, over the whole empire, except Italy itself.

Cassius: In that case, I shall know what use to make of this dagger. Cassius will have no hesitation in freeing himself from such oppression. It is in this way, ye gods, that the weak are endowed with strength, and that the plans of the oppressors are circumvented. Nothing exists strong enough to keep the determined spirit in confinement, neither towers of stones nor walls constructed of hammered brass, nor fetid dungeons, nor iron fetters. If a man is tired of living, nothing whatever can prevent him from taking his own life. Knowing this myself, I am quite willing that everyone else should know it — that it is within my power, at any time, to free myself from the oppression under which I live.

[Thunder still.]

Casca: It is within mine also, and, in this way, every slave has it in his power to set himself at liberty.

Cassius: When such is the case, why does Caesar so tyrannize over us? Still, I pity him. After all, he would not do so if it were not apparent to him that the people of Rome are a poor, spiritless lot. He would not seek to overawe them if they possessed any spirit at all. People who wish to make a big fire quickly, always begin with rubbish, such as straw.

14

What a poor lot the Romans must be, when such a worthless man as Caesar uses them as the base material upon which he may build up his fame and glory! But where is this regret leading me? It may be that I am thus unburdening my mind to one who has no objection to be thus trodden underfoot. In that case, I must answer for my words. Still, I am not quite defenceless and I care not for any dangers I may run.

Casca: You are talking to Casca, and therefore to one who is not in the habit of repeating everything he hears. I give you my hand upon it, I am quite ready to join you in any enterprise you may begin for the remedying of these abuses. I will do as much as anyone else for such a cause.

Cassius: Then we will consider that agreed. I don't mind telling you now, Casca, that I have always persuaded some of the most honorable citizens of Rome to join me in a project that, although not in the least dishonorable, is full of danger. By this time, they will be waiting for me in Pompey's theater, for, on such a terrible night as this, the streets will be quiet and deserted. The dreadfulness of the weather, with its accompaniments of fire and blood, suits the work we have set ourselves to perform.

[Enter Cinna.]

Casca: Let us conceal ourselves. Someone is coming along, evidently in a hurry.

Cassius: Oh, it is only Cinna. I recognize his walk. We need not fear him. Here, Cinna, where are you hurrying to?

Cinna: To look for you. Is that Metellus Cimber who is with you?

Cassius: No, it is someone else who has promised to join us in our project. His name is Casca. Are they not waiting for me, Cinna?

Cinna: I am pleased to hear it. Is it not a terrible night? Some very strange phenomena have been witnessed by some of us.

Cassius: Why don't you answer my question? Are they not waiting for me?

Cinna: Yes, they are. I wish, Cassius, you could induce Brutus to join us.

Cassius: You may rest easy on that point. Here, Cinna, I want you to take this paper and be sure to put it in the chair where Brutus usually sits, so that he cannot help but see it. Take this one and throw it through the window into his room. Fasten this other one with wax on the statue of his great ancestor. When you have done all this, then make your way to Pompey's theater, where we will await you. Have Decius Brutus and Trebonius arrived?

Cinna: They are all there except Metellus Cimber, who has gone to your house to look for you. Well, I will be off and dispose of these papers as you wish.

Cassius: When you have done so, come to Pompey's theater.

[Exit Cinna.]

Now, Casca, before it gets light, let us call on Brutus. Already he is more than half inclined to join us, and very little more persuasion is now needed in order to make him wholly one of us.

Casca: Besides, he is so popular among all classes that what might be considered wrong on our part will appear most honorable and praiseworthy if he but look on it with approval.

Cassius: You are quite right as to the importance of having him on our side. However, we had better be going, for it is already past midnight. Before night is over, we will have our interview with him, and secure his co-operation.

[Exit.]

ACT II • SCENE 1

[Rome. Brutus' orchard.]
[Enter Brutus.]

Brutus: Here, Lucius! It is quite impossible to tell what time of night it is, for the stars are invisible. Lucius! I only wish I could sleep as he does. Here, Lucius, wake up! Don't you hear me?

[Enter Lucius.]

Lucius: Did you call, sir?

Brutus: Light one of the candles in my study, Lucius, and tell me as soon as you have done so.

Lucius: Very well, sir.

Brutus: It is evident that he must die. Personally, of course, I have no reason to bear him any ill will. The welfare of the state is my only consideration. He is, however, evidently aiming at the crown, and the point to be considered is what influence that might have upon him. The snake comes out when the sun is shining, and it is then that we need to be most careful of our steps. It is certain that, if he is made king, we shall be giving him the power of doing great harm if he is so inclined.

The abuse of power lies, of course, in exercising it without regard to mercy, although, to tell the truth, I have never known Caesar to be carried away by his passions. Still, it is a matter of common experience that men often exhibit the greatest humility in order to attain power and influence, but that, as soon as they have attained the height of their ambition, they throw off their false humility and conduct themselves with the greatest pride and arrogance. It may be the same with Caesar, so it will be better not to give him the chance. And, Caesar's character being what it is, as we have no cause for complaint against him, we must argue in this way — that, if he had greater power, he would act in such and such a way. We must, therefore, achieve his destruction while he is still harmless, regarding him as we would a serpent's egg, which becomes a source of danger as soon as it is hatched.

[Re-enter Lucius.]

Lucius: I have lit the candle in your study, sir, and, while I was looking about in the window to find a flint, I came upon this

sealed letter, which I am certain was not there when I
retired to rest.

[Gives him the letter.]

Brutus: Well, you need not stay up any longer; day is not yet
come. Let me see, tomorrow will be the 15th of March, will
it not?

Lucius: I don't remember, sir.

Brutus: Go and look at the almanac, and then tell me.

Lucius: All right, sir.

Brutus: The meteors flashing across the sky will give sufficient
light to read this by.

[Opens the letter and reads.]

"Brutus, you are evidently asleep. Rouse yourself, and
recognize your own worth. Are the Roman people, etc. Let
your voice be heard, remain no longer inactive, but put an
end to the present state of affairs. Wake yourself from your
present lethargy." Ah, words to the same effect have often
been spoken in my own hearing. "Are the Roman people,"
etc. I suppose that means "Are the Roman people to groan
under the tyranny of one man?" The citizens of Rome!
Why, when Tarquin was proclaimed king, he was driven
out of the city by my forefathers. "Let your voice be heard,
remain no longer inactive, but put an end to the present
state of affairs." Do they beg me to raise my voice and to
act? Oh, my countrymen, if it be possible to remedy these
abuses, I promise you I will do everything you ask of me.

[Re-enter Lucius.]

Lucius: I find, sir, that tomorrow will be the 15th.

Brutus: I thought so. I heard someone knocking at the door.
See who it is.

[Exit Lucius.]

Ever since Cassius excited within me these suspicions
concerning Caesar, I have not been able to sleep. The
whole interval between the first suggestion of a terrible
deed and the doing of it appears like a nightmare or a horrible dream. The mental faculties and the bodily powers are
contending with each other, and man's whole state resembles a miniature kingdom suffering from the effects of a
rebellion.

[Re-enter Lucius.]

Lucius: Your friend Cassius is at the door, sir, and says he wishes to speak to you.

Brutus: Is he by himself?

Lucius: No, sir, he is accompanied by several others.

Brutus: Have you any idea who they are?

Lucius: I have not, sir, for their faces were so concealed by their hats and cloaks that there was no means whatever of identifying them.

Brutus: Ask them in.

[Exit Lucius.]

They are evidently the conspirators. O conspiracy, if thou dost not dare to uncover thy ill-favored countenance even in the darkness of night, the time when so much wickedness is abroad, what cave can thou find sufficiently dark to prevent its being seen in the daylight? Thy better plan, after all, is not to seek for any, but to mask thy countenance with smiles and geniality, for if thou goest about in thy natural guise, not even the darkness of Erebus would suffice to prevent thy being seen and recognized.

[Enter the conspirators, Cassius, Casca, Decius, Cinna, Metellus Cimber and Trebonius.]

Cassius: Good morning, Brutus. I am afraid we are interrupting your night's rest. I hope we are not intruding.

Brutus: No, I have not slept at all tonight and have already been up over an hour. Are your companions known to me?

Cassius: Yes, you are well acquainted with all of them. There is not one who has not the highest esteem for you. In fact, they are all unanimous in wishing that you thought as well of yourself as your fellow citizens think of you. Allow me to introduce Trebonius.

Brutus: I am very pleased to meet him.

Cassius: This gentleman is Decius Brutus.

Brutus: I give him a cordial welcome also.

Cassius: This is Casca, this is Cinna, and this is Metellus Cimber.

Brutus: I am very pleased to meet all of them. But what is it that has kept you from your sleep tonight?

Cassius: May I speak with you a moment?

[Brutus and Cassius whisper.]

Decius: Let me see, the east is in that direction, and that is ere we shall see the dawn breaking, is it not?

: I do not think so.

a: Excuse me, sir, it is, and those gray streaks across the clouds show that day is approaching.

Casca: I think I can convince you that both of you are wrong. As it is now springtime, the sun will rise farther to the south, in the direction in which my sword is pointing. In about two months' time, however, it will rise exactly in the east, that is, a little farther north than it does now.

Brutus: Let me clasp each of you in turn by the hand.

Cassius: And we will take a solemn vow.

Brutus: That is not necessary. If the looks on the faces of our fellow citizens, the fears of our own minds and the evils of the present time are not enough to bind us, then let us at once give up our project and each man get back home to his bed, and let this tyrannous oppression continue until, one by one, it is each man's lot to fall. But if, on the other hand, such motives are sufficiently strong — and I feel certain they are — to make even cowards brave and to inspire even weak women with courage, then, my friends, I do not see that anything else is needed to urge us on to the completion of the work we have undertaken than the justice of our own cause. We need nothing else to bind us than the fact that we are citizens of Rome who, their word having been given, will neither draw back, nor betray their companions. Nor do we require any other assurance than that we all, being honorable men, have determined either to accomplish our purpose or lose our lives in the attempt.

Let such oaths be administered to priests, cowards and deceitful men, to those who are aged, weak and contemptible, to those who have not the spirit to stand up for their own rights, and, when cause is unjust, to those whose good faith you may have cause to doubt. But let us not sully the righteousness of our cause or the unquenchable ardor of our souls, by the suggestion that either our project, or our execution of it, requires the incentive of an oath, seeing that no man is worthy to be a citizen of Rome who attempts to break his sworn word in the slightest particular.

Cassius: What shall we do about Cicero? Shall we ask him to join us? He would probably lend us great support.

Casca: Oh, we must certainly not omit him.

Cinna: No, of course not.

Metellus: Yes, we must ask him, for his advanced years will carry weight with the people and tend to bring them over to our side. They will say that he was evidently the prime mover, and our youth and rashness will not be so noticed in the presence of his age and seriousness.

Brutus: Oh, don't mention his name. We had better not broach the subject to him, for he will never have anything to do with schemes initiated by others.

Cassius: We will say no more about him, then.

Casca: Well, really, he is hardly a suitable man.

Decius: Is Caesar the only man against whom our enterprise is directed?

Cassius: That, Decius, is certainly a point to be considered. In my opinion, Mark Antony, who is such a great favorite of Caesar's, ought to share the same fate, for he will prove a mischievous plotter, and his influence, if he chooses to exercise it, may become a source of danger to all of us. To avoid that, it would be as well to rid ourselves of both at the same time.

Brutus: I think that that would be going too far, Cassius. To mutilate a man's body after killing him appears as if one is actuated by feelings of jealousy as well as anger, and Antony, remember, may be compared to one of Caesar's limbs. Let our act resemble the killing of an animal for sacrificial purposes by a priest rather than by a mere butcher. Our enterprise is directed against Caesar's ambitious spirit, and men's spirits are not composed of flesh and blood. It is a matter of deep regret to me that we cannot kill Caesar's spirit without shedding his blood. But it is evident that Caesar must die. And, as it is so, my friends, let us act with boldness, but not as if we sought merely to gratify our own passions. Let us kill him as if we were offering up a sacrifice, not as if we intended to throw his body to the dogs. And, just as clever men often incite their servants to do deeds for which they afterward pretend to scold them, so let our wills deal with our bodily powers. We will so represent our action as to make the populace believe that we were actuated not by jealousy but by patriotism. Thus, instead of being called assassins, we shall be looked upon as deliverers of our country. We will leave Mark Antony alone, for he will be as powerless as Caesar's arm, once Caesar is dead.

Cassius: I am still afraid of him, for all that. When you consider the great regard he has for Caesar —

Brutus: My dear Cassius, put him out of your thoughts. If his regard for Caesar be so great, the most that he could do would be to become melancholy and take his own life. This, however, is scarcely probable, seeing how fond he is of sports, of gaiety and of company.

Trebonius: There is no need to be afraid of him or to put him to death. He will soon get over Caesar's death, and will probably joke about it like the rest of us.

Brutus: Listen! Let us see what the time is.

Cassius: It has just struck three.

Trebonius: It's time we were going.

Cassius: But still, we are not yet certain whether Caesar intends to show himself in public today, for lately his opinions regarding presentiments, dreams and religious observances have so altered from what they used to be, and he has become so superstitious, that it is very probable that these strange phenomena, the unusual severity of tonight's storm, together with the advice that he will most probably receive from his soothsayers, may so influence him that he will decide not to attend the senate house today.

Decius: You need not be afraid of that. Even if he has so decided, I can overrule his decision, for he is fond of being told how easy it is to trap unicorns by pretending to take shelter behind a tree, and bears by placing mirrors in their path, to entrap elephants by digging pits, to catch lions by means of nets and to betray men by flattering them. It is only necessary to tell him that he dislikes flattery for him to immediately say that he does, and for one to see that this is the best way to flatter him. If I do this, I can easily work upon him so that he will come to the senate house.

Cassius: We will make it the business of all of us to see that he does come.

Brutus: Shall we say that eight o'clock is to be the latest?

Cinna: Yes, let that be the latest, and let us all be there prompt.

Metellus: Caius Ligarius, too, has a grudge against Caesar for rebuking him when he spoke in Pompey's praise. I am surprised that his name has not been mentioned by some of you.

Brutus: Well, Metellus, suppose you call upon him. He has a great regard for me, which is not entirely undeserved. If you will tell him to come here, I can easily persuade him to join us.

Cassius: The day is breaking. We will therefore take our departure, Brutus. Now, my friends, let us be going. Do not forget, however, what has been resolved upon. Let it be seen that you are worthy of the name of Romans.

Brutus: Now, gentlemen, see that you put on bright and cheerful countenances. We must not allow our looks to betray us, but carry ourselves with dignified self-possession and unwavering resolution, even as the players do in the theater. I bid you all good morning.

[Exit all but Brutus.]

Lucius! Lucius! Are you sound asleep again? However, it is immaterial. Go on enjoying that deep sleep that is so refreshingly sweet, and, in your case, is undisturbed by any of those imaginary forms or delusions that trouble the sleep of those oppressed with worry and anxiety.

[Enter Portia.]

Portia: My dear Brutus!

Brutus: Why, Portia, what are you doing? Why have you left your bed so early? While you are in so weak a state, it is hardly wise for you to expose yourself to the bleak morning air.

Portia: The exposure will do me no more harm than it will you. It was not very kind of you, Brutus, to leave me in bed by myself. Last evening, too, at suppertime, you abruptly left the table, and, sighing from time to time, walked about the room with your arms folded, as if absorbed in meditation. You looked angrily at me when I ventured to question you as to the reason. I continued to press you on the subject, and still you did not answer, except by scratching your head and impatiently stamping on the floor. At last, on my still urging you, you motioned me away with your hand, as if in anger. I therefore left the room before I should still further stir up your anger. I could see that you were in a bad humor, but hoped that it might prove merely the result of one of those temporary whims to which, at times, every man is liable. But you neither eat your meals nor indulge in conversation nor take your usual rest. If it affected you in your personal appearance much as it has done in these respects, it would be impossible, Brutus, to recognize you. My dear husband, do tell me what it is that troubles you.

Brutus: There is nothing the matter, except that I am not very well.

Portia: You are not devoid of sense, Brutus, and you know very well that, if you were ill, you would employ the right means to become well again.

Brutus: Well, do I not do so? My dear Portia, get back to bed again.

Portia: You say you are not well. Do you mean to tell me that it will do you good to go about with your clothes half-fastened and to inhale the damp morning air? Do you mean to say that, if you were unwell, you would get out of a warm, comfortable bed and expose yourself to the pestilential vapors that rise from the ground during the night, and go the very way to make yourself worse, by going out into the air from which the unwholesome mists have not yet been dispersed? Of course not. The sickness from which you are suffering is some mental trouble, which, as your wife, I am entitled to know. See, I will even go on my knees and beg you, by that beauty of which you used to speak in such praise, by the love you have always professed for me and by our marriage vow by which we were made one, to truly tell me, your wife, what it is that is troubling you, and who the men were that called upon you this evening. Six or seven of them called, and they all kept their faces concealed, although the night was dark.

Brutus: Come, my dear Portia, do not kneel to me.

Portia: If I were your dear Portia, I should have no occasion to do so. Is there any clause in our marriage bond that I am to be kept in ignorance of all your secrets? Am I to be your other self only in some certain manner and with certain restrictions? Am I only to have my meals with you, sleep with you and occasionally converse with you? If I am not to share your inmost thoughts, then I am certainly not your wife, but only your mistress.

Brutus: You are my dear wife, and worthy of all honor and confidence. My own life is not dearer to me than you are.

Portia: If it were so, you would not keep this secret from me. I know that I am only a woman, but I am the one whom you chose to be your wife. And, although only a woman, I am of unsullied reputation and am, besides, the daughter of Cato. Do you think that I am as weak as most women when I have such a father and such a husband? Let me know your plans. They shall not be betrayed by me. See, I have put my firmness to a severe test by deliberately inflicting a wound in my thigh. Do you think I can be able to endure the pain of this without murmuring, and yet be incapable of keeping the secrets of my husband?

Brutus: O heaven, make me fit to be the husband of such a wife.

[Knocking within.]

Listen! Someone is knocking. Go indoors for a little while, Portia, and presently I will tell you all my secrets. I will then fully explain to you everything that has so closely occupied my mind and that has made me look so worried. Do not linger, but go in at once. *[Exit Portia.]* Who is it knocking, Lucius?

[Re-enter Lucius with Ligarius.]

Lucius: A sick man who wishes to speak to you.

Brutus: Why, it is Caius Ligarius, whom Metellus was speaking about. You can retire, Lucius. Caius Ligarius, why, how is this?

Ligarius: I hope you will condescend to accept good morning from a sick man.

Brutus: Well, my dear fellow, you have chosen a very unfortunate time to be sick. I wish you were in perfect health.

Ligarius: I am perfectly well if you are undertaking any enterprise in which honor is to be obtained.

Brutus: Well, Ligarius, if you were only well enough to listen to it, I could tell you about such an enterprise.

Ligarius: Well then, by all the gods of Rome, I herewith cast all my sickness aside. Illustrious Roman! You noble son of a worthy father! Like a sorcerer, you have again revived my drooping spirits. Now tell me what to do, and I will do it, however impossible it may seem to be and whatever obstacles there may be in the way. What is there to be done?

Brutus: Something that will restore health and vigor to those that are sick.

Ligarius: Are there none strong and healthy who need making sick?

Brutus: Yes, there are. However, I will tell you all about it while we are on the way to those, against whom our enterprise is directed.

Ligarius: Start at once, then, and I will follow you with this newly acquired ardor and enthusiasm, although I know not what it is I am going to do. It is quite enough for me that I am following Brutus.

Brutus: Come along, then.

[Exit.]

ACT II • SCENE 2

[Caesar's house.]
[Thunder and lightning. Enter Caesar in his gown.]

Caesar: Both the heavens and the earth seem to have been in a state of commotion tonight. Even Calphurnia herself, while asleep, has called out three times "Help! Help! Caesar is being murdered!" Is anyone in?

Servant: Did you call, sir?

Caesar: Go to the priests and tell them to offer up a sacrifice immediately. Then, come and tell me what you think as to the chances of success.

Servant: Very well, sir.

[Exit.]
[Enter Calphurnia.]

Calphurnia: Caesar, what are you thinking about? Do you still think of going out? I will not allow you to go outside the door all day.

Caesar: I shall go out. I have never yet known any dangers that I was afraid to face, and, as soon as I have faced them, they have invariably disappeared.

Calphurnia: I have never before attached much importance to omens, Caesar, but I am frightened of them now. A person is at present in the house who has been relating some terrible scenes that have been witnessed by the watchmen, in addition to what we ourselves have seen and heard. A lioness has given birth to young ones in the street. The dead have come forth from their graves. Soldiers, clothed in fire and drawn up in correct battle array, have been fighting among the clouds, while their blood fell like rain upon the senate house. The air was filled with the clash of arms, the neighing of horses and the groans of the dying, while the streets resounded with the horrible noises made by the ghosts. All these things, Caesar, are so unnatural that they greatly terrify me.

Caesar: It is impossible to avoid what has already been determined upon by the almighty gods. I shall therefore go out, for these omens refer no more to me personally than they do to the world at large.

Calphurnia: No comets flash across the sky to portend the death of beggars, but, when princes are about to die, the very heavens announce the coming catastrophe.

Caesar: Those who fear danger are continually suffering the pangs of death, but these sufferings are only experienced by the brave once, in the hour of death. I have known many strange things, but I think the most marvellous of all is that men should be afraid, especially when you consider that death is inevitable and that all must die at some time or other.

[Re-enter servant.]

What is the opinion of the soothsayers?

Servant: They strongly advise you not to go out today, for, when they cut one of the animals open, they found it had no heart.

Caesar: The gods evidently brought this about in order that the cowardly might be put to shame. Why, I would be no better than that animal if I allowed fear to keep me indoors today. I am determined to go. Danger himself is well acquainted with the fact that he has no advantage over me. We two resemble lions both born on the same day. I, however, came into the world before danger and am far more to be feared. Therefore, I will not stay at home.

Calphurnia: Alas, my dear husband, you allow your better judgment to be carried away by your rash assurance. If you have no fear yourself, then, oh, respect my fears and let us give Mark Antony a message to take to the Capitol saying that you are ill. Oh, let me entreat you on my knees to grant my request.

Caesar: Very well, we will send the message by Mark Antony and, to please you, I will not go.

[Enter Decius.]

Why, here comes Decius Brutus. He shall take the message.

Decius: Good morning, noble Caesar, accept my greeting. I have come to accompany you to the Capitol.

Caesar: Your coming is opportune. I shall be glad if you will kindly give the senators my compliments, and inform them that I have decided not to come today. It would be untrue to say that it is impossible for me to come, and to say that I am afraid to do so would be still more of an untruth. Therefore, Decius, simply tell them that I am not coming.

Calphurnia: Tell them he is not very well.

Caesar: What, am I to send an untruthful message? Shall I, who have won so many victories, be afraid of telling the truth to a few old men? No, Decius, simply inform them of the bare fact that I am not coming.

Decius: O most illustrious Caesar, will you not give me some reason? They will certainly laugh at me if I give them such a message as that.

Caesar: I do not wish to come, and I have decided not to do so. It must be sufficient for the senators to know that I am not coming. However, as I regard you in the light of a friend, I do not mind telling you, for your own private information, that it is in deference to my wife's wishes that I am not going. She had a dream last night in which my statue appeared to be a fountain having a hundred spouts, from each of which ran blood instead of water. Many of the citizens crowded around it with smiles on their faces and plunged their hands into the blood. She looks upon this dream as an omen and a presentiment of impending danger, and, kneeling before me, has pleaded with me not to go today.

Decius: Why, you have read the dream wrongly. Instead of foreboding evil, it portends good fortune. Your statue appearing as a fountain running blood from so many spouts, in which the people bathed with such evident pleasure, shows that the Roman Empire looks to you to renew her life and that her most distinguished men will court your favor and your smiles. This is the true interpretation of your wife's dream.

Caesar: You have certainly given it a most happy interpretation.

Decius: You will see that I am right when I acquaint you with what is within my knowledge. Listen! It has been resolved by the senate to confer the crown on you today, and it is quite possible they may alter their decision if they receive your message that you do not intend to come. Besides, they might turn it into ridicule and suggest that the senate be adjourned until Calphurnia is favored with better dreams. If you do not appear, they may even say that you are afraid. Forgive me, Caesar. It is the great love I bear you that prompts me to speak as I do, and that overrules my better judgment.

Caesar: Now you see, Calphurnia, how groundless your apprehensions were. It shames me to think that I was in any way influenced by them. Fetch me my robe. I shall not stay at home after all.

[Enter Publius, Brutus, Ligarius, Metellus, Casca, Trebonius and Cinna.]

Why, here is Publius come for me too.

Publius: Good morning, Caesar.

Caesar: I am very pleased to see you, Publius. Why, Brutus, are you up so early also? Good morning, Casca. Ah, Caius Ligarius, the illness that has so reduced you has done you far more harm than I have ever done. What time is it?

Brutus: It is just eight o'clock, Caesar.

Caesar: I am very much obliged to you for the trouble you have taken, and for your kindness.

[Enter Antony.]

Why, even Antony, who usually spends half the night in revelry, is up early this morning. Good morning, Antony.

Antony: I wish you the same, most illustrious Caesar.

Caesar: Tell those within to get ready. I ought not to keep you waiting like this. Now I am ready, Cinna. Come along, Metellus. Ah, Trebonius, is that you? I should like to have a little conversation with you and shall be glad if you will come and see me again presently. Remain close to me, then I shall not be likely to forget the appointment.

Trebonius: Very well, Caesar. *[Aside.]* And I will remain so close that those who love you most will wish that I had not been quite so near.

Caesar: Now, my friends, come into the house, and have a glass of wine with me, and we will then immediately set out together in a friendly manner.

Brutus: *[Aside.]* Ah, Caesar, it grieves me greatly to think that things are so very different from what they appear to be.

[Exit.]

ACT II • SCENE 3

[A street near the Capitol.]
[Enter Artemidorus, reading a paper.]

Artemidorus: Caesar, "I advise you not to trust Brutus. Be suspicious of Cassius. Let not Casca approach you too closely. Keep Cinna under observation. Be wary of Trebonius. Watch Metellus Cimber carefully. You are hated by Decius Brutus, and Caius Ligarius owes you a grudge. All these men have but one purpose, and that is to do you harm. Unless you are invulnerable, it is important for you to be watchful. When there is no suspicion of danger, more opportunity is afforded for the plotting of mischief. May heaven protect you! Your sincere friend, Artemidorus."

I will stay right here until Caesar comes along. Then, I will hand it to him as if it were a petition. It grieves me greatly to think that the virtuous are always in danger from the jealousy of others. O, Caesar, if you will but read this warning, the danger may be avoided, but if thou dost not, then the fates are evidently in league with the conspirators.

[Exit.]

ACT II • SCENE 4

[Another part of the same street, in front of Brutus' house.]
[Enter Portia and Lucius.]

Portia: Here, boy, make your way to the Capitol with all speed. Do not linger even to answer me, but be off at once. What are you waiting for?

Lucius: To learn what I have to do, madam.

Portia: I wish you could have been there and back again before I had time to give you your instructions. Oh, may my fortitude not desert me but enable me to be calm in spite of the perturbation of my soul. My strength of mind is equal to that of a man, but, in other respects, I am only a weak woman. Oh, how difficult it is for a woman not to betray herself! Are you still waiting?

Lucius: I am waiting to know what I have to do, madam. Am I to do nothing more than merely run as far as the senate house, and then come back again?

Portia: Yes, see if your master is looking any better, for he was not very well when he left home. Also, note carefully what Caesar is doing, and who press around him with petitions. Listen, Lucius! What is that noise?

Lucius: I do not hear any, madam.

Portia: Listen intently. It sounded like the noise of tumult and fighting, and appeared to come from the direction of the senate house.

Lucius: Really, madam, I cannot hear anything.

[Enter the soothsayer.]

Portia: Come here, my man. Where have you just come from?

Soothsayer: From my home, madam.

Portia: What time is it?

Soothsayer: It is about nine o'clock, madam.

Portia: Do you know whether Caesar has gone to the senate house yet?

Soothsayer: He has not gone yet, madam. I am just going to take up my position, where I shall be sure of seeing him before he arrives there.

Portia: Have you a request to make of Caesar?

Soothsayer: Yes, madam. If he will only consult his own advantage so far as to listen to me, I shall beg him to have a care for his own safety.

Portia: Why, do you know of any danger threatening him?

Soothsayer: I have no definite knowledge of any, but I am afraid some evil may happen to him. Well, I wish you good day. The street is not very wide just here, and, what with the senators and the magistrates, and those having petitions to present, who always follow in the wake of Caesar's train, the crowd will very nearly crush the life out of a feeble man, who, like me, has not much strength. I must take myself to a more open place and wait there for a chance of speaking to the noble Caesar as he passes.

Portia: Well, I must get indoors again. What weak hearts women have! O Brutus, may the gods assist you in your undertaking! That boy evidently heard what I said. Your master has asked a favor of Caesar that he is unwilling to grant. Oh! A feeling of faintness overcomes me. Hasten, Lucius, and convey my greetings to your master. Tell him that I am in excellent spirits. Then return and let me know what he says.

[Exit separately.]

ACT III • SCENE 1

[Rome, in front of the Capitol. The senate sitting above.]
[A crowd of people, among them Artemidorus and the soothsayer.
Flourish of trumpets. Enter Caesar, Brutus, Cassius, Casca,
Decius, Metellus, Trebonius, Cinna, Antony, Lepidus, Popilius,
Publius and others.]

Caesar: *[To the soothsayer.]* Well, the 15th of March is here.

Soothsayer: Quite so, Caesar. But the day is not over yet.

Artemidorus: I greet you, Caesar! Will you kindly look over this paper?

Decius: Trebonius begs that you will read this, his humble petition, as soon as you possibly can.

Artemidorus: O Caesar, I beg you to look at mine first, for it concerns a matter that affects your welfare very closely. I pray you look at it, noble Caesar.

Caesar: We will leave to the last what affects our own interest.

Artemidorus: O Caesar, read it at once; do not put it off.

Caesar: Has the man taken leave of his senses?

Publius: Out of the way, fellow!

Cassius: Why do you thus press your petitions in public? The senate house is the proper place for that.

> *[Caesar goes up to the senate house, the rest following.]*

Popilius: You have my best wishes for the success of your project today.

Cassius: What do you mean, Popilius?

Popilius: Good-bye.

> *[Advances to Caesar.]*

Brutus: What was Popilius Lena saying?

Cassius: He said we had his best wishes for the success of our undertaking. I am afraid our plot has become known.

Brutus: See, he is making his way toward Caesar. Keep an eye on him.

Cassius: Now Casca, act promptly, otherwise our aim may be frustrated. What had we better do, Brutus? If our plot has been discovered and our scheme fails, then I shall take my own life.

Brutus: Remain firm in your purpose, Cassius. Popilius Lena is not talking about our plans. See, he is smiling, and Caesar remains unmoved.

Cassius: Trebonius is beginning to act. See, Brutus, he has

33

already managed to draw Mark Antony away from Caesar.

[Exit Antony and Trebonius.]

Decius: What has become of Metellus Cimber? It is time he went and presented his petition to Caesar.

Brutus: He is just about to do so. You go and support him.

Cinna: Remember, Casca, you are to strike the first blow.

Caesar: Let the proceedings now commence. What wrongs are there that you wish righted by myself and by my senators?

Metellus: O most noble, most illustrious and most powerful Caesar, before your chair I humbly kneel —

[Kneeling.]

Caesar: I cannot allow you to do so, Cimber. One of the common people might have his heart softened by these bowing and cringing servilities, and, so influenced, he might upset regular legal decisions as if they sprang from childish whims. But do not be so foolish as to think that I am possessed of so weak a will as to be persuaded into altering my mind as a fool might be, by mere flattery, fawning or cringing. Your brother has been exiled by a legal decision. If, therefore, conducting yourself in so servile a way, you come here kneeling and pleading on his behalf, I will treat you with no more consideration than I would a dog. I would have you know that my decisions are always just and that no decree is ever passed without reasonable cause.

Metellus: Will no one who has greater influence with Caesar, plead the cause of my exiled brother?

Brutus: I have no intention of flattering you, Caesar, yet even I humble myself before you and beg that you will recall Publius Cimber's sentence of banishment without delay.

Caesar: You too, Brutus?

Cassius: Forgive me, Caesar, but I also fall at thy feet to plead for the recall of Publius Cimber.

Caesar: If I were an ordinary man like you, I might be persuaded. If I could bring myself to beg of others, I might be affected by their petitions. But I am like the pole star, which always remains immovable in its place, being, in this respect, alone among the stars of heaven. Innumerable stars illuminate the sky, and all are shining fiery globes, but only one, out of all the number, keeps always the same position. It is just the same with the men inhabiting this world. They are very numerous, and they are all similarly formed and of similar intelligence. But, of all the multitude, I know only one that maintains his dignity unaffected by outward influence, and even this matter shall prove to you that I am the one. I was determined to banish Cimber, and I am still as determined to keep him so.

Cinna: I beg thee, Caesar —

Caesar: Away! You may as well attempt to move Olympus.

Decius: Most noble Caesar —

Caesar: Did you not see that even Brutus knelt in vain?

Casca: Let my hands then plead in my behalf.

[Casca first, then the other conspirators and Marcus Brutus stab Caesar.]

Caesar: What, you too, Brutus? Then let me die!

[Dies.]

Cinna: We have freedom and liberty at last. Oppression is over. Delay not, but publish it throughout the whole of Rome.

Cassius: Let some go to the public speaking places and shout "Freedom, liberty and equality for all."

Brutus: There is no reason for fear, fellow citizens and senators. Do not run away. Remain where you are. Ambition has only met with its just reward.

Casca: Mount the rostrum, Brutus.

Decius: Let Cassius do so also.

Brutus: What has become of Publius?

Cinna: Oh, he's here, quite upset by what has occurred.

Metellus: Let us keep close together. It may be that some of Caesar's friends —

Brutus: Oh, don't talk about that. Pluck up courage, Publius. No one wishes to do you any harm, or indeed any other Roman. You may, as well, assure the people on that point, Publius.

Cassius: You had better not remain with us, Publius. Otherwise, if we are attacked by the mob, you may receive some injury.

Brutus: No, do not stay. We do not wish anyone else to suffer from the consequences of our action.

[Re-enter Trebonius.]

Cassius: What has become of Antony?

Trebonius: He ran home in terror. All the people, too, are shrieking and rushing about with scared faces, as if it were the day of judgment.

Brutus: It is a matter of anxiety to all, as to what the future may have in store for us. We are aware that death is inevitable, but we all desire that that hour may be delayed as long as possible.

Cassius: But the shortening of a man's life by 20 years only shortens, in the same degree, the period during which he is living in fear of death.

Brutus: If we admit the truth of that, then death must be considered as an advantage. In that case, by shortening the period during which Caesar would have lived in fear of death, we have done him a kindness. Come, my countrymen, let us stoop down and smear the blood of Caesar over our hands, our arms and our swords, then let us go to the forum and, waving our blood stained swords in the air, shout, "peace, liberty and freedom."

Cassius: Yes, let us bend down and bathe our hands. Think how, in after ages, this dignified scene of ours will be re-enacted in languages as yet unspoken and among nations yet unconstituted!

Brutus: And how often in plays shall be acted the death of Caesar, whose dead body, of no more value than the soil of the earth, now lies at the foot of Pompey's statue?

Cassius: Well, each time that that happens, we shall be looked upon as the saviors of our country.

Decius: Are we to show ourselves in the streets?

Cassius: Yes, let us all go. We will make Brutus our leader, and we, the bravest and noblest in Rome, will follow him.

[Enter a servant.]

Brutus: Hush! Let us see who it is that approaches. It is evidently one of Antony's friends.

Servant: O Brutus, I come to throw myself at your feet, in obedience to the commands of Mark Antony, my master, by whom I was commissioned to say, while on my knees, that Brutus possesses nobility of spirit and wisdom, that he is also brave and honorable, while Caesar was great and bold and possessed both dignity of spirit and kindness of heart. Antony has both love and esteem for Brutus, but, while possessing the same love and esteem for Caesar, he also held him in some fear. If Brutus will guarantee that Antony shall not suffer any harm in coming to him, and will satisfy him that Caesar merited his death, then Mark Antony will consider that the living Brutus is more worthy of his regard than the dead Caesar, and will not hesitate to throw in his lot with the illustrious Brutus, and give him what assistance he can in the present unsettled state of affairs. This is the message I bring from Antony, my master.

Brutus: Your master is evidently what I always considered him to be, a Roman citizen distinguished for both wisdom and bravery. You can inform him that if he cares to come here, I will satisfy his doubts, and that I pledge my word that he shall be allowed to come and go in perfect safety.

Servant: I will tell him, and he will probably come immediately.

[Exit.]

Brutus: I am sure that he will come over to our side.

Cassius: I hope he will. Still, I cannot say that I wholly trust him, for I am still afraid he may stir up mischief.

Brutus: Well, here he is.

[Re-enter Antony.]

I am pleased to see you, Mark Antony.

Antony: O Caesar, hast thou so fallen from thy greatness? Is this all that now remains of all thy victories, thy honors and thy trophies? Well, I bid thee good-bye. Now, sirs, I have no idea of your present intentions, whether anyone else is to be slain, or has attained too great influence in your opinion. If I am to be the next victim, then no time can be more suitable than that of Caesar's death, and no weapon more desirable than those swords of yours, which are already stained with the lifeblood of the noblest man in the world. If, therefore, you have any grudge against me, I beg of you to carry out your intentions at once, while the blood on your hands is still wet and warm. However long I live, I shall never be more prepared for death than I am now. Nor could I wish to die in any more agreeable place than here by the side of Caesar, nor in any other way than at your hands, seeing that you now possess the greatest power and influence in Rome.

Brutus: O Antony, do not ask to die at our hands. Although our appearance and the deed we have just committed may cause us to appear both cruel and bloodthirsty, still you can only see our bloody hands and the dead body of Caesar. You do not know the reason that prompted us. We were actuated solely by pity for the wrongs done to the Roman people. Just as one kind of fire is driven out by another, so our pity for the people nerved our hearts to show no pity to Caesar. As for you, Mark Antony, we have no quarrel with you. We have no wish to do you any harm, and we therefore welcome you as a brother, with all brotherly affection, kindliness of spirit and esteem.

Cassius: Well, after all, you are as suitable a man as any to be at the head of affairs.

Brutus: If you will only have patience until we have pacified the people, who are almost out of their minds with terror, we will then explain to you our reasons and why I, who had so much regard for Caesar, should thus have lifted my hand against him.

Antony: I have no doubts as to the expediency of your course. Let me clasp each of you by the hand, although they are stained with blood. I will take your hand first, Marcus Brutus. I will shake hands next with you, Caius Cassius. And next with you, Decius Brutus. Now give me yours, Metellus. I will now clasp yours, Cinna, and now yours, brave Casca. And, although I take yours last, Trebonius, do not think that I hold you in any less esteem than the others. Now, sirs — alas, I know not what to say. My position just now is such that I must either be suspected of cowardice or of cringing servility.

O Caesar, I must admit that you were very dear to me. If it is possible for thy spirit to see us now, the sight of thy Antony fraternizing with those who bore thee such ill will, and clasping their bloodstained hands in his, even by the side of thy dead body, must cause thee greater sorrow than even thy murder. Were my eyes as numerous as thy wounds, it would be far more suitable were tears to flow as copiously from them all as the blood is now flowing from thy wounds than for me to be thus making friends with thy foes. Forgive me, Caesar. Here, like a gallant animal, thou wast driven to bay, and it was here that thou met with thy death. Round thee stand those who hunted thee down. The whole world constituted the forest in which thou wandered, the noblest of all its inhabitants. Oh, as thou liest there, what a great resemblance there is between thee and a deer hunted to its death by noble and illustrious men!

Cassius: What means this, Mark Antony?

Antony: I crave your forgiveness, Caius Cassius. What I have said will be admitted even by Caesar's foes, therefore it can hardly be considered out of place on the part of a friend.

Cassius: I have no wish to chide you for so speaking in Caesar's praise, but what is your attitude toward us? Are we to count upon you as one of us, or are we to proceed with our plans without your aid?

Antony: I shook hands with you to show that I was on your side, but, seeing the body of Caesar, my emotion carried me away. I have no wish to be unfriendly, for I have the greatest regard for all of you. I am hoping, however, that you will justify your deed by telling me why, and for what reasons, Caesar was to be feared.

Brutus: If we could not, it would have been a brutal murder. But we have such good reasons for our deed, Antony, that you would agree to its justice, even if Caesar had been your own father.

Antony: I wish to know no more. I beg, however, that you will give me permission to carry Caesar's body to the forum, and to say a few words from the rostrum, as a friend should do, during the funeral ceremony.

Brutus: You have our full permission, Mark Antony.

Cassius: Brutus, I should like to speak to you for a minute. *[Aside to Brutus.]* You are making a mistake. Do not allow Antony to say anything during Caesar's funeral. You do not know what he may say, nor what effect his words may have upon the people.

Brutus: Excuse me, but I shall mount the rostrum myself first, and explain why Caesar was put to death, and I will assure them that whatever Antony says, is said with our full knowledge and authority, and that we have no wish for Caesar's funeral to be conducted otherwise than with all due rites and religious observances. It will do us good rather than harm.

Cassius: I am not at all certain as to the result. I would rather it were not to be.

Brutus: Here, Mark Antony, we leave Caesar's body in your hands. Remember, in this funeral oration of yours, you are not to cast any blame upon us. Say all you can in praise of Caesar, and tell them that you have our full authority for doing so. Otherwise, you will not be allowed to take any part whatever in the ceremonies. Your speech, too, shall be delivered from the same rostrum from which I intend to speak, but I will address the people first.

Antony: Very well. I have no wish that it should be otherwise.

Brutus: See that the body is laid out properly and then come with us.

[Exit all but Antony.]

Antony: O my slain friend, forgive me for acting in so mild and submissive a manner toward thy murderers. Thou liest there, the remains of the most illustrious man the world has ever known. May disaster overtake those who murdered thee! Here, even in the presence of thy bloody wounds, which appear like mouths pleading with dumb eloquence for me to speak in their behalf, do I predict that men shall be afflicted with bodily plagues, that there shall be quarrelling in the home and that the whole of Italy shall be embroiled in war. Deeds of violence and blood shall become so common, and people shall become so familiar with terrible sights that mothers shall look on with indifference, even if their children are being hacked to pieces by the sword and their finer feelings are being blunted by the frequency of such atrocious cruelties. The soul of Caesar, roaming about in search of vengeance, in company with the spirit of revenge that shall come in hot haste from the lower world, shall, with the authority of a monarch, cause these territories to be ravaged by fire, by famine and by the sword, until the whole earth shall be polluted by the bodies of the unburied dead, as the result of this cruel and wicked deed.

[Enter a servant.]

You are one of Octavius Caesar's servants, are you not?

Servant: Yes, Mark Antony.

Antony: Caesar sent him a letter, requesting his presence at Rome.

Servant: Caesar's message was duly received by Octavius, and he is now on his way. I am commissioned by him to tell you personally — alas, Caesar! —

[Seeing the body.]

Antony: You have a tender heart. Do not restrain your tears, but step aside a moment. Sorrow is infectious, and the sight of your tears bring tears into my own eyes. Did you say your master was on his way?

Servant: His resting place tonight will be within 20 miles of Rome.

Antony: Return as quickly as possible and acquaint him with what has occurred. Hasten back at once and tell him that Rome is overwhelmed with sorrow, and that he will incur great danger if he sets foot in Rome at present. After all, I think you had better wait until Caesar's body has been taken to the forum, for I intend to sound out the people during my speech there and see what they think of the brutal deed just committed. Then, you will be able to tell Octavius exactly how things stand. Give me your assistance.

[Exit with Caesar's body.]

ACT III • SCENE 2

[The forum.]
[Enter Brutus, Cassius and a throng of citizens.]

Citizens: We must know the meaning of all this. Give us an immediate explanation.

Brutus: Well, come with me, friends, and listen to my explanation. Cassius, you take some of them into the other street. Now, let those who wish to hear what I have to say remain here, and those who would rather hear Cassius, accompany him. We will then publicly explain why Caesar has been put to death.

First Citizen: I will listen to Brutus' explanation.

Second Citizen: I will see what Cassius says. Then, having heard both, we shall be able to judge how far they agree.

[Exit Cassius, with some of the citizens. Brutus goes into the pulpit.]

Third Citizen: Let all be still. The illustrious Brutus is in the rostrum.

Brutus: Have patience with me until I have finished speaking. People of Rome, my fellow citizens and friends, I beg that you will grant me a hearing, for the sake of the cause I have to plead, and that you will not interrupt me. I pray you, for

41

the sake of my honorable character, to believe that what I say is true and to let my known character weigh with you in judging me. Wisely form your own opinions and bring all your intelligence to bear upon the facts in order that your decisions may be the more accurate and just. If there is anyone in my audience to whom Caesar was especially dear, let me inform him that he could not regard Caesar with more affection than I did. If then I am asked why I am found among the number of his foes, my reply is that my affection for Rome was far greater than even my love for Caesar.

Would you prefer that Caesar should still be living and that you should be in a state of slavery all your lives, or that Caesar should be dead and that you should be in the enjoyment of liberty and freedom? As Caesar regarded me with affection, I mourn his death. Since he was possessed of bravery, I respected and esteemed him. But, as he was aiming at too much power, I took his life. I weep because he loved me. I rejoiced when he was fortunate. I respected his bravery, and I killed him because he wished to be supreme. Is there anyone present who is so low and vile that he would willingly live in a state of slavery? If so, let him come forward, for I have gravely displeased him. Is there one so uncivilized that he takes no pride in being a Roman? If so, let him also come forward, for I have also incurred his displeasure. Is there one so mean and worthless that he has no love for his native land? If so, let him come forward likewise, for I have equally displeased him. I await an answer.

All: There is no one, Brutus.

Brutus: In that case, I have displeased no one. I give you liberty to do the same with me, as I have done to Caesar. The circumstances of Caesar's death have been duly recorded in the senate house. The honor and renown that were deservedly his have not in any way been depreciated, nor have the faults that led to his death been exaggerated.

[Enter Antony and the others, with Caesar's body.]

See, his body is already being brought here, accompanied by the sorrowing Antony, who, although he took no part in slaying him, will share as equally in the advantages accruing from his death as the rest of you will. I will say no more except that, since I put my dearest friend to death for the benefit of my country, I am perfectly willing to lay down my own life whenever it shall be in the interests of Rome to do so.

All: We do not desire thy death, Brutus.

First Citizen: Let us form a triumphal procession and escort him home.

Second Citizen: Erect a statue in his honor, like those of his ancestors.

Third Citizen: Put him in Caesar's place.

Fourth Citizen: The nobler qualities of Caesar shall then find their reward in Brutus.

First Citizen: We will cheer him all the way home.

Brutus: Fellow citizens —

Second Citizen: Hush, be quiet! Brutus is speaking.

First Citizen: Silence there!

Brutus: My fellow citizens, do not attempt to follow me, but do me the favor of remaining here with Antony. Show honor to the dead body of Caesar and give Antony your respectful attention while he speaks what he can in Caesar's praise, which we have given him our full authority to do. I beg that no one will leave, with the exception of me, until Antony has finished his speech.

[Exit.]

First Citizen: We will remain and hear what Antony has to say.

Third Citizen: Let him mount the rostrum, and we will give him a hearing. Get up into the pulpit, illustrious Antony.

Antony: I am very much obliged to you for so readily granting Brutus' request.

[Goes into the pulpit.]

Fourth Citizen: What was that remark he made about Brutus?

Third Citizen: He said that he was very much obliged to us for agreeing to Brutus' request.

Fourth Citizen: He had better not say anything against Brutus in my hearing.

First Citizen: Caesar's rule was certainly becoming oppressive.

Third Citizen: There is no doubt about that. It is fortunate for us that it is now at an end.

Second Citizen: Don't talk any more! Let us give Antony our attention.

Antony: My fellow citizens —

Citizens: Silence! Give us a chance of hearing him.

Antony: Citizens of Rome, my fellow countrymen and friends, give me your attention. I am not here to speak in praise of Caesar, but to bury him. Men's evil deeds are remembered long after they themselves are dead, but their good ones are often forgotten as soon as they are buried, and there is no reason why it should not be so even in the case of Caesar. You have been told by the illustrious Brutus that Caesar was aiming at too much power. If this is true, then it was a serious failing on his part, and his punishment has been equal to the offence. I am here to say a few words during Caesar's funeral ceremonies by permission of Brutus and his friends. I may say that Brutus is actuated solely by principles of honor, as indeed all of them are. I looked upon Caesar as a dear friend, and I always found him loyal and true. Still, we have it on the word of Brutus that he aimed at greater power, and Brutus is one whose word commands respect.

Many prisoners have been brought by Caesar to Rome, and, when they were ransomed, the money was thrown into the public treasury. Was that a sign of such ambition on Caesar's part? The sufferings and hardships of the poor have always caused Caesar great grief — an ambitious man is not usually so tender-hearted. Still, we are told by Brutus, that this was Caesar's great failing, and we must certainly believe what Brutus says. You, yourselves, were witnesses on the feast of Lupercalia that I offered him the crown three times, but that each time he put it aside. Did that look as if he were ambitious? Still, we have been told by Brutus that he was, and we cannot believe that Brutus is moved by any unworthy motives. I do not say all this to prove that Brutus is wrong, but to tell you of those things that are within my own knowledge. There was a time when Caesar was held dear by all of you, and, as you know, there were ample reasons for it. Why, then, should you not now grieve for his death? O discernment, thou hast evidently abandoned thy usual dwelling place and taken up thy home in the breasts of wild animals, for men seem to have lost their power of reasoning. Be not impatient with me. The sight of Caesar lying there in his coffin overcomes me, and I must wait a moment in order to regain my self-composure.

First Citizen: It appears to me that there is something in what he says.

Second Citizen: Well, after all, when you come to think of it, Caesar has evidently been treated very unjustly.

Third Citizen: Do you think so, gentlemen? I am afraid that we shall not find his equal to succeed him.

Fourth Citizen: Did you notice what he said? Caesar refused the crown. It seems evident, therefore, that he was not so anxious for more power.

First Citizen: If that can be proved, someone will have to suffer for this deed.

Second Citizen: Poor fellow! He has shed so many tears that his eyes are all inflamed.

Third Citizen: Antony is certainly the most worthy man in Rome.

Fourth Citizen: Listen! He is going on with his speech again.

Antony: Only a few hours ago Caesar's word was law throughout the world. Now he lies in his coffin, and there is no one who will condescend to show him the slightest respect. Gentlemen, if I had any wish to excite your passions or to rouse you to rebellion, I should be doing an injustice to Brutus and also to Cassius, both of whom are known to you all as men of irreproachable honor. They shall not suffer such an injury at my hands. I would rather be unjust to the dead Caesar, to myself and you, than to men whose characters are so upright and free from blame. See, I have here a paper that I discovered in Caesar's study, bearing his seal and containing directions for the final disposition of his property. I have no intention of reading it, but, if the people only knew its contents, they would caress the very wounds on Caesar's body and soak up his precious blood with their handkerchiefs and would consider themselves fortunate if they could obtain but a single hair of his head to preserve as a sacred memorial of him, and, when they died, would make special mention of it in their wills, leaving it to their children as a priceless heirloom.

Fourth Citizen: Tell us the terms of the will. We want to know what they are, Mark Antony.

All: Yes, read the will! We are determined to know what it contains.

Antony: My dear friends, restrain your impatience. It would be wrong for me to read it. It is better that you should remain in ignorance of Caesar's great love for you all. You are not inanimate or unfeeling objects, but human beings. Since you possess human feelings, the hearing of Caesar's will would rouse your passions and stir up the fury of your wrath. It is far better that you should not know that he has left all his property to you, otherwise I do not know what the result would be.

Fourth Citizen: Let us hear the will, Antony. We will know what is in Caesar's will, and we insist upon hearing it.

Antony: Calm yourselves, my friends, and have patience for a little while. It was indiscreet on my part to mention it. I am afraid I am doing an injustice to those worthy men who put Caesar to death. I am very much afraid of it.

Fourth Citizen: Worthy citizens indeed! I call them treacherous villains.

All: Read the will. Let us hear the will.

Second Citizen: They were scoundrels and assassins. Tell us the terms of the will. We want to know what is in the will.

Antony: You insist, then, on my reading the will? Well, stand round Caesar's dead body, and you shall first see the man who drew up the will. Have I your permission to come down?

All: Yes, we give you permission.

Second Citizen: Come down.

Third Citizen: You have our full permission.

Fourth Citizen: Now then, form a circle.

First Citizen: Don't stand so near the platform, go farther away.

Second Citizen: Leave a space for the illustrious Antony.

Antony: Come, do not crowd round me like this. Stand farther back.

Several Citizens: Don't stand so close. Make room. Go farther back, there.

Antony: If you are not utterly devoid of feeling, this sight should bring the tears to your eyes. This cloak is familiar to all of you. The first occasion on which it was worn by Caesar is still fresh in my mind. He put it on in his tent in the evening of that summer's day on which he defeated the Nervii. See, this is the hole made by Cassius' weapon, and this large one was made by the jealous Casca. This one shows where he was stabbed by the dearly loved Brutus. See how Caesar's blood issued from the wound when the cursed weapon was withdrawn, as if in haste to see whether it was really Brutus who had dealt so cruel a blow, for as is well-known to all of you, Caesar looked upon Brutus as his good guiding spirit, and only heaven knows the depth of Caesar's affection for him.

Not one of the other stabs was so cruel as this one. When the illustrious Caesar perceived him among his assailants, he was utterly overcome by his ingratitude, which proved more powerful than even the dastardly blows of his enemies. His noble heart was broken, and, covering his face with his robe, the noble Caesar fell at the foot of Pompey's statue, down which the blood was pouring all the time. My fellow citizens, it was the greatest calamity that could happen to us. The death of Caesar is the ruin of us all, and the murderous traitors are exulting over our undoing. Ah, now your eyes are wet with tears, and it is evident that pity has at last touched your hearts, for your very tears prove your kindly feelings. But does the mere sight of Caesar's mutilated robe thus bring tears to your eyes? See here then, here see him, himself, covered with wounds inflicted by traitors.

First Citizen: Oh, what a sorrowful sight!

Second Citizen: Alas, that he should come to this!

Third Citizen: It was indeed a calamitous day.

Fourth Citizen: Oh, the treacherous scoundrels!

First Citizen: Is it not a gory spectacle?

Second Citizen: His death shall be avenged.

All: We will have vengeance. Let us set to work at once and find the traitors. We'll put them all to death and set fire to their houses.

Antony: Wait, my fellow citizens.

First Citizen: Silence! Give the illustrious Antony your attention.

Second Citizen: He shall have our attention, and he shall be our leader, even to death, if necessary.

Antony: My good, kind friends, do not let my words be the cause of so hasty an outburst of rebellion on your part. The perpetrators of this deed are men of principle and honor. I regret that I am not able to tell you what personal grievances they may have had that led them to this act, but, as they are of irreproachable character and possessed of wisdom, they will, I dare say, give you good and sufficient reasons for it. I am not here, my friends, to win you over to my way of thinking by working on your feelings. I am not possessed of Brutus' eloquence, but, as is known to all of you, am an unpolished, straightforward man who regarded Caesar with affection. This fact is also well-known to those by whom I have been thus permitted to say these few words in his praise. It is not in my power to move men's hearts by either my ingenuity or my eloquence, for my words, being ill-chosen, carry no weight. My manner of speaking, also, is faulty and unrelieved by appropriate gesture. I merely say whatever occurs to me and inform you of those things with which you are already acquainted. I direct your attention to the gaping wounds on poor Caesar's body and leave them to plead with you in their dumb eloquence. If, however, I possessed the ability of Brutus, I could so work upon your feelings and passions as to rouse you to the highest pitch of excitement and fury, and so elaborate upon the wrongs that Caesar has thus suffered that the very stones in the streets would be moved by my eloquence to protest against this cruel deed.

All: We will rise in rebellion.

First Citizen: Let us set fire to Brutus' house.

Third Citizen: We will go at once and find the traitors.

Antony: My fellow citizens, listen to me. Allow me to say a few more words.

All: Silence all! Listen to the most illustrious Antony.

Antony: Look here, my friends, you have no idea where your feelings are leading you. What has Caesar done to merit such action on your part? Ah, you are still in ignorance, and it obliges me to inform you. Just now, I made mention of Caesar's will, but it seems to have passed from your memories.

All: You are quite right. Read the will. We will not go until we have heard it.

Antony: Well, this is it, and, as you see, it bears the seal of Caesar. He bequeaths to each citizen of Rome, that is, to each man, 75 drachmas.

Second Citizen: O most illustrious Caesar! His death shall be avenged.

Third Citizen: Most generous Caesar!

Antony: Have patience and listen to me.

All: Silence, silence!

Antony: Besides that, he has bequeathed to you and to your descendants, in perpetuity, all his pleasure grounds, his summer houses and the orchards that he recently had planted on this side of the river Tiber. They are to be thrown open for the equal enjoyment of all of you, so that you can ramble about in them and refresh yourselves when tired and wearied. Here you see a man worthy of his name. It will be long before we meet another so noble.

First Citizen: We shall never do so. Let us go at once and burn his body in the place reserved for this sacred rite. Then, we will take some of the burning wood and set fire to the houses of the villains. Carry the body away.

Second Citizen: Bring some lighted sticks.

Third Citizen: Tear up some of the seats.

Fourth Citizen: Break up and bring anything that will burn.

[Exit citizens with the body.]

Antony: We shall now see the effects of my speech. Well, mischief, as I have now started thee, it matters little to me in what form thou showest thyself.

[Enter a servant.]

What is your business, my man?

Servant: Please sir, Octavius has already arrived in Rome.

Antony: At whose house is he staying?

Servant: He is staying at Caesar's house, with Lepidus.

Antony: I will go at once and see him. I had just been wishing for his arrival. Fortune is evidently in a good humor and will, no doubt, grant us whatever we may wish at the present moment.

Servant: He mentioned, in my hearing, that Brutus and Cassius had been seen riding furiously through the city gates.

Antony: Perhaps the news had reached their ears of the effect my speech had upon the people. Conduct me to Octavius.

[Exit.]

ACT III • SCENE 3

[A street.]
[Enter Cinna the poet.]

Cinna: Last night, I had a dream in which I thought I was at a banquet with Caesar, and my mind, in consequence, is burdened with ominous fancies. I have no desire to go outdoors, and yet I feel as if I am compelled to do so.

[Enter citizens.]

First Citizen: By what name are you known?

Second Citizen: What is your destination?

Third Citizen: In what street do you live?

Fourth Citizen: Have you a wife, or are you unmarried?

Second Citizen: Reply to each of our questions in a straightforward manner.

First Citizen: Yes, and let your answers be to the point.

Fourth Citizen: And mind you answer intelligently.

Third Citizen: Yes, and it will be to your advantage to tell the truth.

Cinna: What name do I bear? Where am I bound? Where is my residence? Am I married or single? Well, my replies shall be straightforward, short, sensible and truthful, as you require. Well, my first answer shall be sensible at any rate. I am not married.

Second Citizen: I suppose that means that sensible men do not get married. All right, I'll owe you something for that. Go on. Now for a straightforward one.

Cinna: I am just off to see Caesar's funeral ceremonies.

First Citizen: Out of friendship or because you bear him ill will?

Cinna: Out of friendship.

Second Citizen: Well, that reply is straightforward enough.

Fourth Citizen: Now a short answer. Where do you live?

Cinna: Well, to be short, I live close to the senate house.

Third Citizen: Now, truthfully, what are you called?

Cinna: To tell you the truth, I am called Cinna.

First Citizen: Fall upon him. Show him no mercy. He is one of the traitors.

Cinna: My name is certainly Cinna, but I am the poet of that name.

Fourth Citizen: Well then, kill him because he writes such rubbishy poetry.

Cinna: I am not the Cinna that plotted against Caesar.

50

Fourth Citizen: Well, he is called Cinna, at all events. Tear his name out of him and send him about his business.

Third Citizen: Yes, kill him, put him to death! Now, then, get your firebrands, and let us be off to the houses of Brutus and Cassius. Set fire to all their houses. Some of you make your way to the dwelling of Decius, others to that of Casca and others to that of Ligarius. Let us be off at once.

[Exit.]

ACT IV • SCENE 1

[A house in Rome.]

[Antony, Octavius and Lepidus seated at a table.]

Antony: All these men whose names we have picked are to be put to death.

Octavius: Your brother, Lepidus, must also be put to death. Are you willing for this?

Lepidus: I am quite willing —

Octavius: Very well, Antony, mark his name.

Lepidus: Provided, Mark Antony, that your nephew, Publius, also dies.

Antony: All right then, he shall die. See, I condemn him by picking his name. Now, Lepidus, I want you to make your way to Caesar's residence and bring the will here. We will then see whether we cannot reduce some of the bequests.

Lepidus: Why, shall you be here when I return?

Octavius: Yes, or if I am not here, you will find me at the senate house.

[Exit Lepidus.]

Antony: He is an insignificant man and utterly devoid of merit. He is only fit to run on errands. Do you think him worthy to be allowed to share with us in the division of the empire?

Octavius: Well, you had no doubts about it a little while ago, when we drew up our fatal list of condemned persons, you asked his opinion as to whom should be condemned to death.

Antony: You see, Octavius, I am older than you, and although we may share these distinctions with Lepidus in order that we ourselves may be less tainted with blame, still, he will only resemble a donkey laden with gold. The only result will be that he will have all the worry and trouble connected with his share, and will, moreover, be compelled to conduct himself according to our wishes until he has served our purpose. We can then deprive him of them, just as we relieve the donkey of his burden and turn him loose to do whatever he pleases.

Octavius: Well, do as you please in the matter, but do not forget that he has proved himself a brave soldier.

Antony: My horse has done the same, and, on that account, I always see that he has a plentiful supply of food. He is simply an animal whom I have taught the various movements required in warfare. He turns, or halts or goes straightforward, but whatever he does is performed in accordance with my will. And, to a certain extent, Lepidus is similar to my horse, for we shall have to teach him what to do and make him do it. He is incapable of originating anything himself, and is quite satisfied with castaway and broken fragments, things abandoned as worthless, and with aping the manners of others. These, when discarded and made common through their continued use by others, are taken up by him as the newest fashion. In fact, we need only consider him as a mere instrument that we are using for our own purposes. We will now speak of more important things, Octavius. Brutus and Cassius are raising troops, and it is necessary that we should at once show them a bold front. Let us, therefore, closely unite together all those who belong to our party, make as many friends as we can, and use our wealth to the best advantage. Let us consult at once as to the best way of discovering any secret plotting against us, and as to the most effective way of meeting and overcoming those dangers that are openly threatening us.

Octavius: We cannot do better, for we are like bears tied to a stake and surrounded by hounds clamoring to set upon us. I am afraid that some who are openly siding with us are secretly plotting against us.

ACT IV • SCENE 2
[A camp near Sardis. In front of Brutus' tent.]
[Drumming. Enter Brutus, Lucilius, Lucius and soldiers.
Titinius and Pindarus meet them.]

Brutus: Who comes there?

Lucilius: Halt! And give the password.

Brutus: What news do you bring, Lucilius? Will Cassius soon be here?

Lucilius: Yes, he is now not far off, and he has commissioned Pindarus to bring you words of greeting.

Brutus: I am glad to hear it. I don't know whether it is because of a change for the worse in his own disposition or the misconduct of his subordinates, but, certainly, Pindarus, some of his recent acts have been such that I could not possibly approve of them. However, if he is now on his way here, I shall soon have a full and satisfactory explanation.

Pindarus: I have no fear but that you will be satisfied that my illustrious master is still possessed of proper feeling and that he has acted only from honorable motives, as he really has.

Brutus: I do not suspect him of having acted otherwise. Lucilius, I wish to speak to you. What reception did you meet with at his hands? I want to be quite sure as to his attitude toward us.

Lucilius: Well, he received me with the utmost politeness and civility, but he did not show those proofs of familiarity or that unstudied ease and intimacy in his conversation as he used to do.

Brutus: That is evidently because his friendship is cooling. You will always notice, Lucilius, that people act with the most studied politeness when their affection is beginning to grow cold. Those who are genuine and sincere have no need of artificial display. But those who are insincere resemble horses that, being hard to hold because of their eagerness, appear to be high-spirited and look as if they are capable of both speed and endurance, but which, as soon as they are called upon to respond to the spur, droop their heads and, like worthless animals, fail miserably when put to the test. Are his troops far away?

Lucilius: They intend camping tonight at Sardis. Most of them and, in fact, the whole of the cavalry are already here with Cassius.

[Low march within.]

Brutus: Listen! Here he comes. Let us go on slowly and meet him.

[Enter Cassius and his attendants.]

Cassius: Halt!

Brutus: Halt there! Pass the order on down the ranks.

First Soldier: Halt!

Second Soldier: Halt!

Third Soldier: Halt!

Cassius: My illustrious friend, you have treated me with injustice.

Brutus: As heaven is my judge, I do not even treat my foes with injustice. Therefore it is impossible for me to do an injustice to a friend.

Cassius: Your very gravity, Brutus, shows that you are, even now, harboring thoughts about me that ought to have no existence, and when you treat me so unjustly —

Brutus: Calm yourself, Cassius, and tell me your grievances quietly. Remember, your disposition is well-known to me. Do not let us quarrel in the presence of our respective troops, for they, at least, ought not to suspect but that we are the best of friends. Dismiss them for the present and then come into my tent. There, you can set forth your grievances fully, and I will patiently listen to what you have to say.

Cassius: Pindarus, give orders to the officers to lead their men a little farther away.

Brutus: You do the same, Lucilius, and then see that no one approaches our tent until our conference is ended. Give orders for Lucius and Titinius to mount guard outside the door.

ACT IV • SCENE 3

[Brutus' tent.]
[Enter Brutus and Cassius.]

Cassius: Now, the following fact proves that you have treated me with injustice. Lucius Pella has been condemned and branded with disgrace, by your orders, for accepting bribes from the inhabitants of Sardis. Although I wrote to you, begging you not to punish him, knowing as I did his honorable character, you treated my letters with contempt.

Brutus: It was unworthy on your part to attempt to excuse such an offence.

Cassius: It is not advisable, at times like these to deal with every trifling indiscretion as hardly as it might deserve under other circumstances.

Brutus: You may as well know, Cassius, that people are saying that even you are not above accepting bribes for placing incompetent and unworthy men in positions of trust.

Cassius: I accept bribes! If you were not Brutus, you would not dare to thus accuse me, or, by heaven, I would never give you the chance of speaking so again.

Brutus: And it is only because this bribery is associated with the name of Cassius that it does not meet with its well-deserved punishment.

Cassius: Punishment!

Brutus: I should advise you not to forget what happened on the 15th of March last. Was it not in the cause of justice that the noble Caesar was put to death? Was there one of those who plunged their daggers into his body that was such a scoundrel as to do so for any other reason but that of justice? Are we, who took it upon ourselves to put the greatest man in the empire to death for merely lending his approval to tyrannous oppression, to demean ourselves by accepting bribes and to barter our honor and our dignity for a mere handful of gold? Why, even a dog is not so contemptible as a Roman who is capable of such acts as these.

Cassius: Do not irritate me, Brutus, for I will not stand it. What right have you to dictate to me as to my actions? Remember that my experience in military matters is greater than yours, and that, therefore, I am far more capable of deciding such questions.

Brutus: I am as well able to judge as you are.

Cassius: I do not think so.

Brutus: Well, I say I am.

Cassius: Do not provoke me further, or I shall be unable to restrain myself. I advise you, if you have any regard for your well-being, not to anger me further.

Brutus: Get out of my way, you worthless fellow.

Cassius: What, do you use such insulting language to me?

Brutus: Listen to me, for I am determined that you shall hear what I have to say. Am I to allow your headstrong wrath to have its own way? Do you think I am to be cowed by the mere glance of a lunatic?

Cassius: Good heavens! Am I expected to submit to these insults?

Brutus: Yes, and more also. You shall chafe under them until your pride shall be humbled to the dust. Keep these outbursts of temper for such times as you are in the presence of your slaves. Then, you can show off your authority if you like, but do not imagine that I am going to watch your moods or that I am going to get out of the way of your wrath. I am not to be awed by such exhibitions of passion. I swear by heaven that you may get rid of your anger as best you can, however disagreeable you may find it to do so, for, henceforth, when you are in such an irritable state of mind,

I shall look upon you as a source of merriment and as an object for ridicule.

Cassius: Have matters come to such a state as this?

Brutus: You state that you have a better knowledge of military matters. Well, show it. If you can prove the truth of your boast, I shall be only too pleased, for I am always willing to be taught by abler men.

Cassius: You do me injustice in every way. I assure you, Brutus, that you judge me wrongfully. I did not say that I had a better knowledge, but that I had had much longer experience. At any rate, I do not remember saying that I had a better knowledge.

Brutus: It makes no difference whether you said that or not.

Cassius: Caesar, when he was living, would never have dared to provoke me as you have done.

Brutus: Silence! You know very well that you would never have dared to try his patience so.

Cassius: I should never have had the courage?

Brutus: You would not.

Cassius: Do you mean to say that I would have been afraid to do so?

Brutus: It would almost have been more than your life was worth to do so.

Cassius: You had better not take too much advantage of my friendship, otherwise I may be led to do something that I may regret later.

Brutus: You ought to regret the deeds you have already committed. I am not at all frightened, however, by your menaces, for I am so conscious of my own honorable motives that they have no more influence upon me than the wind, of which I take no notice. I requested you to forward me some money, but you refused to do so. I will not stoop to despicable means for raising money. Why, by the gods of Rome, I would sooner turn my own heart into gold and coin every drop of my blood into drachmas, than extort money by dishonorable means from toiling peasantry. I asked you to remit me some money in order that I might pay the troops, and you refused to do so. Was such an action worthy of Cassius? Do you think I should have acted so if Cassius had asked me for such money? If I should become so avaricious as to refuse my friends the loan of a few worthless pieces of metal, I hope the gods will strike me dead.

Cassius: I did not refuse to send you the money.

Brutus: You said you would not do so.

Cassius: I never sent such a message. The bearer of it, in his stupidity, must evidently have misrepresented what I said. It grieves me greatly to think you have such an opinion of me. Friends ought to make allowances for each other's weaknesses. You, however, exaggerate mine.

Brutus: On the other hand, I overlook them altogether until you begin to make me the subject of them.

Cassius: You are evidently no longer my friend.

Brutus: It is your faults that I dislike.

Cassius: If you were really my friend, you would not notice them.

Brutus: One who wished to flatter you would pretend not to do so, however great they might be.

Cassius: O Antony and Octavius, I would you two were present, and that I, singly, might bear the whole brunt of your vengeance, for I am tired of life. My friend no longer loves me, but treats me with contempt. I am dictated to, as regards my actions, as though I were a slave. All my failings are noted and recorded. They are learned by heart and treasured up to be used against me. Really, I could almost die of grief. Here, take this weapon. See, I bare my breast. Within it, there beats a heart more valuable than all the wealth in the treasure house of Plutus, and more to be prized than the most precious of metals. If you are worthy of the name of Roman, accept the sacrifice. I, who would not give you money, will give you my life. Plunge the dagger into my breast as you did into that of Caesar, for I am sure you had more affection for him, even at the time when you were most opposed to him, than you ever had for Cassius.

Brutus: Put your weapon away. For the future, your anger shall have free play. Whatever you do, however dishonorable it may be, shall be regarded merely as a whim of the moment. Ah, Cassius, you will find, after all, that your colleague is one who is naturally as gentle as a lamb and whose anger, even when provoked, lasts but a moment and is then over.

Cassius: Have I indeed come to this, that I am to be an object of merriment and of ridicule to you whenever my hasty temper or my troubles happen to put me in a bad humor?

Brutus: Well, I also was in a bad humor when those words escaped me.

Cassius: Do you really admit that? Then, let us shake hands.

Brutus: And let us forget our differences.

Cassius: Ah, Brutus!

Brutus: Why, what ails you now?

Cassius: Is not your friendship for me sufficiently great to enable you to have patience with me when my natural hastiness of temper, which I inherited from my mother, causes me to forget my good manners?

Brutus: It is, Cassius, and, for the future, whenever you lose your temper with me, I will consider that it is your mother's hastiness showing itself, and I will not attempt to provoke you further.

Poet: *[Within.]* I must have an interview with the commanders. It is not safe to leave them by themselves, for there is ill-feeling between them.

Lucilius: *[Within.]* You cannot go in.

Poet: *[Within.]* Only death shall prevent me.

        [Enter poet, followed by Lucilius, Titinus and Lucius.]

Cassius: Now then, what is all this about?

Poet: You commanders ought to be ashamed of yourselves for quarrelling in this way.

        Let friendship and love be between you two;
        Just take my advice, I am older than you.

Cassius: Just listen what wretched rhymes this fellow makes.

Brutus: Take yourself off, sir. Be off at once, you impudent rascal.

Cassius: Do not be impatient with him, Brutus, it is only his way.

Brutus: I will make allowance for his "way," then, when he recognizes the proper season for indulging in it. Such foolish writers of doggerel are quite out of place in times of war. Away, fellow!

Cassius: Be off at once! Away you go!

                      [Exit poet.]

Brutus: Lucilius and Titinius, let the officers be told to get quarters ready for their troops.

Cassius: Then both of you return at once to us, and tell Messala to come with you.

[Exit Lucilius and Titinius.]

Brutus: Fetch me a glass of wine, Lucius.

[Exit Lucius.]

Cassius: I should not have believed that it was possible to so rouse your anger.

Brutus: Alas, Cassius, I have so many troubles to worry me that I am quite upset.

Cassius: Well, if you thus give way under mere chance misfortunes, you evidently do not derive much advantage from your philosophical habit of mind.

Brutus: Well, I do not think anyone could bear trouble more calmly than I do. My wife is no longer living.

Cassius: What! Is Portia dead?

Brutus: I am sorry to say that she is.

Cassius: Then I wonder you did not slay me when I gave you so great provocation. Oh, how deeply you must feel her loss! What was the cause of her death?

Brutus: Well, being unable to endure my absence and, grieving because Octavius and Antony had raised such a large body of troops, — news of which reached me at the same time as that of her death — her mind became unhinged and, in the absence of her maids, she swallowed some burning coals.

Cassius: And was this the way in which she died?

Brutus: It was.

Cassius: Good heavens!

[Re-enter Lucius with wine and a candle.]

Brutus: Let us not dwell on this subject. Hand me a glass of wine. In this, Cassius, I drink to the renewal of our affection.

[Drinks.]

Cassius: It is the one thing I most desire. Lucius, fill the glass to the brim. It is impossible for me to have too much of Brutus' affection.

[Drinks.]

Brutus: You may enter, Titinius.

[Exit Lucius.]
[Re-enter Titinius, with Messala.]

I am pleased to see you, Messala. Let us now sit round this light and discuss what it is necessary for us to do.

Cassius: And art thou really dead, Portia?

Brutus: I beg you not to refer to that subject again. Information has reached me, Messala, that Octavius and Antony are bearing down upon us with a powerful army and that they are marching in the direction of Philippi.

Messala: Information to the same effect has also reached me.

Brutus: What other news have you?

Messala: I am also informed that 100 members of the senate have been executed after being condemned and outlawed by Octavius, Antony and Lepidus.

Brutus: As regards that, my information differs slightly. I am told that 70 have thus been condemned and put to death, including Cicero.

Cassius: What, has Cicero been condemned?

Messala: Yes, and put to death.

Did you receive the letters you expected from Portia, my lord?

Brutus: I have heard nothing from her, Messala.

Messala: And was nothing said about her in the letters you did receive?

Brutus: Her name was not mentioned, Messala.

Messala: I am surprised at that.

Brutus: Why do you put the question? Was she mentioned in the letters you received?

Messala: She was not, my lord.

Brutus: Come, tell me the truth, on your honor as a citizen of Rome.

Messala: Well then, may you bear with a Roman's strength the news I bring. She is dead, and her death happened very strangely.

Brutus: Then I wish thee good-bye, Portia. Death comes to all of us, Messala, and the thought that her death must have happened at one time or another enables me to bear it with strength now.

Messala: It would be well if all great troubles were borne by great men in the same way that you bear them.

Cassius: I, like you, Brutus, profess to be a Stoic, but I would not be able to bear such tidings as you do.

Brutus: Well, let us who are still alive resume our business. What is your opinion as to an immediate march to Philippi?

Cassius: It seems to me that it would be inadvisable.

Brutus: Why so?

Cassius: For this reason. Our wisest plan would be to remain where we are until our foes come up to us. In this way, they will be exhausting their supplies, wearying their troops and, so, injuring themselves. We, on the other hand, as a result of our inaction, besides resting ourselves, remain strongly defended and ready for immediate action whenever it is required.

Brutus: Your arguments are sound, but I think better reasons can be urged in favor of my proposal. The inhabitants of the district between here and Philippi are not very well disposed toward us. We have had great difficulty in obtaining supplies. If we allow our foes to pass through this district, their numbers will be recruited from the people, and they will advance against us in great force and with renewed strength and vigor. But, if we march on to Philippi, and there engage them, we shall, by leaving this unfriendly district in our rear, deprive them of this advantage.

Cassius: Listen to me, my friend.

Brutus: Excuse me a moment. You must remember, also, that we have already obtained all the assistance that it is possible for our friends to give us. Our plans are fully matured, and we have no hope of further adding to our troops. We therefore run the risk of decreasing in strength, while, on the other hand, our foes are continually adding to their numbers. Every man, at some time or other during his lifetime, has an opportunity to improve his fortunes in the future by taking advantage of the favorable circumstances by which he is then surrounded. If he neglects to do so, no other such chance of improvement ever again presents itself. Such an opportunity has now come to us, and our enterprise will certainly end in failure if we do not take advantage of it.

Cassius: Well, if that is your conviction, let us set out. We will march at once to Philippi and there engage them.

Brutus: Night has stolen upon us while we have been talking, and we had better take a little sleep, for we cannot afford to disregard the claims of nature. Is there anything further to discuss?

Cassius: There is nothing else. Good night. We will get up early in the morning, and set out.

Brutus: Lucius! *[Enter Lucius.]* Fetch me my dressing gown.

[Exit Lucius.]

Good-bye, Messala. I wish you good night, Titinius. Good night Cassius, my illustrious friend, and may you sleep well.

Cassius: Ah, my beloved friend, how badly we began the evening! Never again let such differences occur between us, Brutus.

Brutus: Well, we are friends again now.

Cassius: I wish you good night, Brutus.

Brutus: Good night, my dear friend.

Titinius: ⎫
Messala: ⎭ Good night, your excellency.

Brutus: I wish you all good-bye.

[Exit all but Brutus.]
[Re-enter Lucius with the gown.]

Hand me that dressing gown. Have you got your musical instrument?

Lucius: I have it here, sir.

Brutus: Why, you talk as if you were sleepy. Well, my poor lad, I will not scold you. You are evidently worn out with staying awake so long. Tell Claudius and some other man of my guard to come here. They shall have some cushions and sleep in my tent tonight.

Lucius: Claudius and Varro!

[Enter Varro and Claudius.]

Varro: What is your pleasure, my lord?

Brutus: I want you, gentlemen, to sleep in my tent tonight. Very likely I shall have to call you presently to take a message to Cassius, my colleague.

Varro: If you wish it, sir, we will remain standing and wait until you require us.

Brutus: No, I do not wish you to do that. You shall sleep for a while. Possibly I may change my mind. Ah, Lucius, I have found the book that I was looking everywhere for. It was in the pocket of my dressing gown.

[Varro and Claudius lie down.]

Lucius: I was certain I had not received it from your lordship.

Brutus: You must excuse me, my lad, I have a very bad memory. Do you think you could keep awake long enough to play a tune or two on your instrument?

Lucius: Yes, sir, if you wish it.

Brutus: Well, my lad, I should like you to do so. I ought not to give you so much trouble. You are always ready to fulfil my wishes.

Lucius: It is only what I ought to be, my lord.

Brutus: Still, I ought not to expect work from you when you are not in a fit state to do it. The young and healthy always require a certain amount of rest.

Lucius: I have already had some sleep tonight, sir.

Brutus: You were very wise. You shall go to bed again presently. I shall only keep you a short time. If I live, you shall be rewarded.

[Music and a song.]

Well, there is not much life in that tune. Thou cruel sleep, dost thou thus stupefy the senses of my boy, who was entertaining thee with sweet music? Good night, my dear boy, I will not treat you so unkindly as to interrupt your slumbers. Your slightest movement, however, may cause the fall and consequent breakage of your instrument. I will therefore relieve you of it. Good night, my dear lad. Now, I wonder where I left off reading. I fancy I turned the page down. Ah, I suppose this is it.

[Enter the ghost of Caesar.]

What a bad light this candle gives! Whatever is this thing that approaches me? It must surely be the dimness of my sight that conjures up and gives shape to this terrible appearance. It draws nearer and nearer. Hast thou any real existence, or art thou merely an illusion? Art thou divine, art thou a heavenly messenger or art thou some demon, that thus terrifies me and causes my hair to stand on end? Tell me, what is thy nature?

Ghost: I am your evil genius.

Brutus: What object hast thou, in thus visiting me?

Ghost: I come to inform you that we shall meet again at Philippi.

Brutus: Oh, all right. Then you intend to visit me again?

Ghost: Yes, at Philippi.

Brutus: Very well, then, we will resume our acquaintanceship at Philippi.

[Exit ghost.]

Ah, thou disappearest now that I have recovered from my fright. Thou evil spirit, I should like to have further conversation with thee. Lucius! Varro! Claudius! Wake up, all of you. Claudius!

Lucius: It is the fault of the strings, my lord. They are out of tune.

Brutus: He fancies he is still playing. Wake up, Lucius.

Lucius: Yes, sir?

Brutus: What made you cry out, Lucius? Were you dreaming?

Lucius: I was not aware that I made any noise.

Brutus: You certainly did do so. Did you witness anything strange?

Lucius: No, sir.

Brutus: Well, go to sleep again, Lucius. Now Claudius, sir, *[To Varro.]* and you fellow there, wake up!

Varro: Yes, sir?

Claudius: Did you call, sir?

Brutus: What made you both utter such cries while you were asleep?

Varro: ⎱ We did not know that we did, sir.
Claudius: ⎰

Brutus: Well, you did do so. Did you see anything strange?

Varro: Nothing has been seen by me, sir.

Claudius: Nor by me, sir.

Brutus: Well, I want you to go to my friend, Cassius, with my greeting and tell him to put his troops in motion early in the morning. We will then bring up the rear.

Varro: ⎱ Your commands shall be obeyed, sir.
Claudius: ⎰

[Exit.]

ACT V • SCENE 1

[The plains of Philippi.]
[Enter Octavius, Antony and their army.]

Octavius: Well, Antony, what we were wishing for has come to pass after all. You were of the opinion that our foes, instead of descending to the plain, would remain entrenched among the hills. They have not done so, for their divisions are now approaching. They evidently intend to take the initiative and to offer us battle here at Philippi, even before we thought of challenging them.

Antony: Nonsense! I know their intentions, and I understand the reason that prompted them. They would be very glad to change their position. They come down with a terrible display, imagining that by presenting a bold front, they will impress us with the idea that they are full of bravery. But such is not the case.

[Enter a messenger.]

Messenger: Commanders, get ready. Our foes are advancing in brave array. They have already donned their scarlet coats, and immediate action is necessary.

Antony: Octavius, you take the left side of the level plain, and let your division advance slowly.

Octavius: No, I am going to lead the right wing. You take the left.

Antony: What reason have you for thwarting my wishes at so critical a time?

Octavius: I have no wish to thwart you, but I am determined to lead the right wing.

[March.]
[Drum. Enter Brutus, Cassius and their army; Lucilius, Titinius, Messala and others.]

Brutus: They are halting. They evidently wish to talk with us.

Cassius: You remain here, Titinius. We must go forward and confer with them.

Octavius: Shall the signal be given for engaging, Mark Antony?

Antony: Not yet, Caesar. We will not engage them until they make their attack. Go forward. Their commanders desire to confer with us.

Octavius: Do not attempt to advance until the order be given.

Brutus: So, my countrymen, we are to have talking before fighting, are we?

Octavius: It is not because we resemble you, in preferring words to deeds.

Brutus: Kind words are certainly to be preferred to unkind blows, Octavius.

Antony: Certainly, but you are in the habit of dealing unkind blows even while you are speaking your kind words. See, for instance, how you stabbed Caesar to the heart, even while you cried "I greet you, Caesar, live forever!"

Cassius: No one yet knows the character of the blows you are capable of dealing, Antony, but, as far as your words are concerned, they are so soft-spoken and so sweet that one cannot help thinking you must have visited the bees of Hybla and stolen all their honey.

Antony: Well, I have not stolen their stings, at any rate.

Brutus: Yes, you have, and you have evidently deprived them of their buzzing powers also, for you very prudently give us warning of your intention to sting.

Antony: Well, you scoundrels gave no such warning when your detestable weapons met and clashed in Caesar's body. You grinned like so many apes, you resembled dogs in your fawning and you cringed before Caesar, caressing his feet, as if you were his slaves, while the accursed Casca, like a cowardly mongrel, stabbed Caesar in the back. You fawning hypocrites!

Cassius: Fawning hypocrites! You now see, Brutus, the result of your absurd leniency. If my advice had been followed, we would not have been thus insulted today.

Octavius: Let us waste no more time, but get to business. If our argument thus causes so much heat, the proving of it will evidently end in blood. See, my sword is drawn, in order to be used against traitors. When do you think it will be sheathed again? Not until I have taken vengeance for the 33 wounds received by Caesar, or until a second Caesar has met his death at the hands of traitors.

Brutus: There is no possibility, Caesar, of treachery claiming you as a victim, unless it already exists among your own followers.

Octavius: Well, I hope not. It was not intended that I should meet my death at the hands of Brutus.

Brutus: Well, young man, it would be impossible for you to die a more honorable death even if you were the most illustrious descendant of your race.

Cassius: A foolish stripling like him, the companion of one who spends his time at the theater, and in riotous celebrations, is undeserving of such an honor.

Antony: I see, Cassius, you are just as ill-tempered as you used to be.

Octavius: Let us leave them, Antony. We defy you, traitors. If you have sufficient courage to risk a battle at once, we will engage you. If you have not, we will wait until you feel brave enough.

[Exit Octavius, Antony and their army.]

Cassius: Well, it does not matter how the winds may blow, or how the waves dash against the vessel, so long as it remains afloat. The tempest is already beginning to rage, and everything now depends on chance.

Brutus: Here, Lucilius, I want to speak to you.

Lucilius: *[Standing forth.]* Yes, sir?

[Brutus and Lucilius converse apart.]

Cassius: Messala!

Messala: *[Standing forth.]* What are your orders, sir?

Cassius: Today is my birthday, Messala. This is the anniversary of the day on which I first saw the light. Shake hands with me, Messala. You shall bear me testimony that in my case, as in Pompey's, it is with the greatest reluctance that I find it necessary to stake the whole success of our enterprise upon the result of a single battle. You are aware that I have always been a firm believer in the doctrines of Epicurus, but now I renounce them, and am inclined to believe in presentiments and omens. During our march from Sardis, a couple of immense eagles landed on our foremost banners and remained sitting there, taking and eating their food from the hands of the soldiers. They followed us all the way to Philippi, but this morning they took off and disappeared. Now, carrion birds are hovering over us, as if we were dying men, and they were waiting to prey on our dead bodies. It almost appears as if our troops, overshadowed by these birds, lie under a canopy at the point of death.

Messala: Do not give way to such thoughts.

Cassius: Well, I do not wholly believe in them, for my spirits are not at all depressed, and I am determined to boldly face whatever dangers may present themselves.

Brutus: You are quite right, Lucilius.

Cassius: Well, most illustrious Brutus, let us hope that heaven will be on our side today, so that after the turmoil of war is over, we may enjoy peace and rest, and go on to old age in uninterrupted friendship. But, as all things in this life are so uncertain, it will be wise for us to prepare ourselves for the worst. If we are not victorious in this battle, we shall never again have an opportunity of talking to one another. What do you intend to do?

Brutus: Well, in exact accordance with the principles of that philosophy that induced me to condemn Cato for committing suicide — for, somehow or other to thus anticipate the time when life naturally comes to an end, simply from fear of what may happen, always appears to me to be a base and cowardly act — I am determined to await the period preordained by those superior powers, by whom the destinies of men are governed.

Cassius: Then, in the case of our defeat, you would have no objection to being taken back to Rome by Antony and dragged through the streets at his chariot wheels?

Brutus: I would not submit to that, Cassius. Do not imagine, my illustrious friend, that I will ever be taken back to Rome in chains, for I possess too much pride to suffer such an indignity. We must, however, finish today the work we began on the 15th of March. It may be that this is the last time we shall ever be together. We will therefore bid each other an eternal farewell. Good-bye, my friend, forever. If we should both survive this day, well, we shall make merry over it; if it happen otherwise, we could not have parted in a better way.

Cassius: Well, good-bye forever, Brutus. As you say, we will make merry over it if we both survive, but, if not, it is well that we part as we do.

Brutus: Let us not linger further. I wish, however, it were possible to know, beforehand the result of today's engagement. After all, we must be satisfied to know that the day will not last forever, and that we shall know the result as soon as the day is ended. Let us be off.

[Exit.]

ACT V • SCENE 2

[The field of battle.]
[A call to arms.]

Brutus: Ride with all speed, Messala, and carry these orders to the divisions of the other wing. *[Loud call to arms and battle sounds.]* Tell them to attack immediately. The troops under the command of Octavius do not appear very eager for the fight, and it is possible that an unexpected attack may result in their utter defeat. Ride with all possible speed, Messala, and let all the divisions advance at once.

ACT V • SCENE 3

[Another part of the field.]
[Sounds of battle. Enter Cassius and Titinius.]

Cassius: Look, Titinius, see how the rascals are running away! I have acted as an enemy to some of my own soldiers. My standardbearer here was beginning to flee. I therefore killed the coward and took the standard out of his hand.

Titinius: Ah Cassius, Brutus ought not to have been so hasty in giving the signal for engaging. There was the chance of obtaining an advantage over Octavius, and he was too hasty in securing it, for his troops then devoted themselves to plunder, the result being that Antony has succeeded in surrounding our wing.

[Enter Pindarus.]

Pindarus: Retire, your excellency, retire to a greater distance. Your camp has been taken by Mark Antony. O most illustrious Cassius, flee from here at once.

Cassius: We need not go any farther than this hill. Look there, Titinius, where those flames are rising! Is that my camp?

Titinius: Yes, it is, your excellency.

Cassius: If you have any regard for me, Titinius, take my horse and ride with all possible speed as far as that body of troops over there. Then return at once and inform me whether they are friends or foes.

Titinius: I shall be back immediately.

[Exit.]

Cassius: You, Pindarus, climb to the top of the hill. My eyesight was never very good. Keep your eye on Titinius and inform me of anything else that you see going on.

[Pindarus ascends the hill.]

This is the anniversary of my birth. The circle of my life has been completed, and the same day that saw my birth will see my death. My days are ended. Well, sir, what have you to tell me?

Pindarus: *[Above.]* Alas, your excellency!

Cassius: What do you see?

Pindarus: *[Above.]* Titinius is surrounded by men on horse-back, who are advancing upon him at full speed, but he does not stop. Now they have almost reached him. Make an effort, Titinius! Some of them are dismounting. Ah, he is doing the same. They have captured him. *[Shout.]* Listen! They are shouting in triumph.

Cassius: Do not look any longer, but descend. Alas, how devoid of courage I am, to have lived so long as to allow the one who loved me most to be taken prisoner, almost in my very presence!

[Pindarus descends.]

Come here, sir. You were taken prisoner by me in Parthia, and, in return for sparing your life, I made you swear that you would do your best to execute whatever orders I might give you. Now is the time for you to fulfil your promise and to gain your freedom. Take this trusty sword, with which I helped to kill Caesar, and plunge it into my breast. Do not wait to reply. Take the sword by the han-dle and run it through me as soon as I cover my face like this. *[Pindarus stabs him.]* The very weapon that caused thy death, Caesar, has avenged it.

[Dies.]

Pindarus: Thus I have secured my freedom. Still, I would not have gained it in this way had I been free to refuse. Ah, Cassius, I will remove myself to a distant land where no Roman will ever recognize me.

[Exit.]
[Re-enter Titinius, with Messala.]

Messala: It is only one of the chances of war, Titinius, for the illustrious Brutus has defeated the troops of Octavius, just as Antony has defeated those of Cassius.

Titinius: Cassius will be glad to hear it.

Messala: Where was he when you left him?

Titinius: I left him, sad and sorrowful, on this hill in company with his slave, Pindarus.

Messala: Does that not look like him, lying there on the ground?

Titinius: My heart frightens me. The way in which he is lying is not the way in which a living man would lie.

Messala: But it is he, is it not?

Titinius: It was, Messala, when he was alive, but he is dead. O sun, as thou settest this evening, bathed in ruddy splendor, so has the sun of Cassius' life set, bathed in his own red blood. With him, the glory of Rome has perished, and all that made the day of our life pleasant and enjoyable has now passed away. Night is approaching, with all its accompanying discomforts and perils. Our work is ended. It was doubt as to the result of my errand that caused him thus to put an end to his life.

Messala: Yes, it was doubt as to the successful result of it that caused it. Thou detestable error, thou offspring of melancholy, what reason hast thou for acting on the susceptible minds of men to make them conceive things that have no existence? Thou art readily formed, but thy birth is always unlucky, for thou always cause the death of that parent by whom thou art conceived.

Titinius: Why, what has become of Pindarus? Pindarus!

Messala: See if you can find him, Titinius. I will make my way to Brutus and wound him with this news. I use the word "wound," because he would as soon be wounded by a dagger or a poisoned arrow as hear what has happened to Cassius.

Titinius: Away you go then, Messala, and I will see if I can find Pindarus.

[Exit Messala.]

O valiant Cassius, why was I sent on such an errand? Were they not your friends that I encountered? Was I not commissioned to bring you back this garland, in token of their victory? Did not their shouts reach your ears? Alas, you misinterpreted all that happened. Here, let me place this wreath on your head. I was told by Brutus, himself, who loved you so, to bring it to you, and I now fulfil his request. Hurry, Brutus, and witness what love I have for Caius Cassius. Pardon me, O heaven. It suits a Roman — thus do I plunge the sword of Cassius into my own bosom.

[Kills himself.]

[Sounds of battle. Re-enter Messala, Brutus, young Cato, Strato, Volumnius and Lucilius.]

Brutus: Well, where is the body of Cassius lying?

Messala: It is over there, and Titinius is weeping over it.

Brutus: But Titinius is lying on his back.

Cato: And he is dead.

Brutus: Ah, Julius Caesar, thy authority and influence are not yet at an end. Thy spirit still roams the earth and directs our weapons against our own selves.

[Low sounds of battle.]

Cato: Noble Titinius! See, he has placed the wreath on Cassius's brows, even though he is dead.

Brutus: Surely, we shall never again find two such Romans! Thus, Cassius, I bid thee good-bye, the last of thy race, for another such illustrious Roman could not possibly be born. My friends, it would be impossible for you to conceive what grief I feel at this man's death. But, my Cassius, if tears can express it, I will spend my time in weeping. Let us cause his body to be taken to Thasos, for it would cause great disorder in our camp if we performed his funeral ceremonies here. Come along, Lucilius, and you also, Cato; we will return to the field. Now, Flavius and Labeo, we will set our troops in motion. It is now three o'clock. Before the sun sets, we will see the result of another engagement.

[Exit.]

ACT V • SCENE 4

[Another part of the field.]

[Sounds of battle. Enter fighting, soldiers of both armies. Then Brutus, young Cato, Lucilius and others.]

Brutus: Now, my countrymen, do not be discouraged.

Cato: Only the cowardly would be. Come, follow me! And all shall hear that my name is Cato, that Marcus Cato was my father, and that, like him, I am ready to oppose the oppressor and to fight and die for the liberties of my country.

Brutus: And I, also, have the welfare of my country at heart, for my name is Marcus Brutus.

[Exit.]

Lucilius: What! Hast thou fallen, Cato, thou so youthful and yet so brave? Well, in thy death, thou showest as great courage as did Titinius, and hast shown thyself worthy of thy father.

73

First Soldier: Surrender or I kill thee.

Lucilius: Well, I surrender on condition that you do kill me. Here, I will give you this money if you will put me to death at once.

[Offering money.]

I am Brutus, and it will bring you honor to slay me.

First Soldier: No we have been ordered to take you alive, for you are a distinguished captive.

Second Soldier: Make way, there! Carry the news to Antony that Brutus is captured.

First Soldier: I will inform him. See, he is approaching.

[Enter Antony.]

We have captured Brutus, your excellency.

Antony: What have you done with him?

Lucilius: He has escaped you, Antony. You may rest assured that the illustrious Brutus will never allow himself to be taken alive, by any foe. May heaven protect him from so great an indignity! Wherever he be found, whether living or dead, you will never find him acting anything but a noble part.

Antony: You have mistaken your man, my friend. Still, you have taken a prisoner quite as distinguished. Don't let him escape, but treat him with all due courtesy. I would far rather have men like him on my side than against me. Well, proceed, and find out whether Brutus is living or dead. Then, make your way to the tent of Octavius, and tell us all that has happened.

[Exit.]

ACT V • SCENE 5

[Another part of the field.]

[Enter Brutus, Dardanius, Clitus, Strato and Volumnius.]

Brutus: Come, you, who are the only one left of my once numerous friends, and sit here by me.

Clitus: The signal agreed upon was given by Statilius, but he has not returned, your excellency. I fear he has either been captured or slain.

Brutus: Well, take a seat, Clitus. He has doubtless been slain, for killing appears to be the prevailing custom at present. Clitus, I have something to say to you.

[Whispering.]

Clitus: Do you ask me to do such a thing, my lord? I would not do so for any consideration.

Brutus: Very well, say no more about it.

Clitus: I would far sooner take my own life.

Brutus: Listen to me, Dardanius.

[Whispering.]

Dardanius: Do you think me capable of doing such a thing?

Clitus: Ah, Dardanius!

Dardanius: Alas, Clitus!

Clitus: What dreadful deed did Brutus ask you to do?

Dardanius: He asked me to slay him, Clitus. See, he is now in deep thought.

Clitus: He is so stricken with sorrow that he is even weeping.

Brutus: Volumnius, come here, my friend. I wish to speak to you.

Volumnius: What is it, your excellency?

Brutus: Well, the matter stands thus, Volumnius. I have seen Caesar's spirit on two separate occasions, each time at night. I saw it first at Sardis, and I saw it again last evening, here at Philippi. The hour of my death is at hand.

Volumnius: Do not say so, your excellency.

Brutus: I have not the slightest doubt about it, Volumnius. You can see for yourself how matters stand. We have been driven by our foes to the edge of the abyss *[Low sounds of battle.]*, and it is far braver for us to voluntarily take the final plunge than to wait until we are thrust over by them. Volumnius, my friend, you remember that we were schoolfellows together. Therefore, for the sake of our lifelong friendship, I ask you to hold the handle of my sword, while I throw myself upon it.

Volumnius: That is hardly the part for a friend to take, my lord.

[Sounds of battle.]

Clitus: Flee, your excellency. It is impossible to linger here.

Brutus: I bid you all good-bye. Ah, Strato, you have been asleep for some time. I bid you good-bye, also. Well, my countrymen, I rejoice to say that, during my whole life, I have never found anyone disloyal to me. This day's disaster, however, will bring me far more honor than their miserable success will ever bring to Octavius and Antony. I will lose no more time in bidding you good-bye, for almost my last words have now been spoken. This is the only result of all my labors, and I now feel the need of repose and rest.

[Sounds of battle. Cry within, "flee, flee, flee!"]

Clitus: Oh, your excellency, flee at once.

Brutus: Go on, and I will come directly.

[Exit Clitus, Dardanius and Volumnius.]

Strato, I would like you to remain behind with me. You deserve to be treated with regard, and your life has not altogether been a dishonorable one. Hold this sword for me, and look in another direction while I fall upon it. Are you willing to do this, Strato?

Strato: Shake hands with me first. Good-bye, my lord.

Brutus: Good-bye, Strato. *[Runs on his sword.]* Caesar, may thou now rest in peace! I felt far greater reluctance in slaying thee than I do in taking my own life.

[Dies.]

[Sounds of battle. Retreat. Enter Octavius, Antony, Messala, Lucilius and the army.]

Octavius: Who is that man?

Messala: He is one of my master's servants. What has become of your master, Strato?

Strato: He has escaped the captivity in which you are now held, Messala. All that his enemies can do now is to burn his dead body. Brutus was conquered by himself only, and no one else can boast of having killed him.

Lucilius: Well, it is a suitable end for him. I am glad, Brutus, that you have thus verified my words.

Octavius: I will take into my own service all those who were formerly in that of Brutus. Are you willing to serve me, my man?

Strato: Yes, if Messala will recommend you to take me.

Octavius: I wish, then, you would do this, Messala.

Messala: What was the manner of my master's death, Strato?

Strato: He asked me to hold his sword for him, and then he fell upon it.

Messala: Then, Octavius, I recommend you to take as one of your followers the man who performed the last kindness for my master.

Antony: Of all the citizens of Rome, he was the greatest and the most distinguished. He was the only one of the conspirators who was not motivated by jealousy of Caesar, and the only reason he joined them was because he really thought that he would be promoting the welfare of the state. His disposition was most amiable, and, in fact, his whole character was such that nature could boldly face the world and proclaim that he was a true man.

Octavius: Well, we will treat him with all honor and give him those funeral ceremonies that his virtues deserve. His dead body shall rest tonight in my tent, laid out with all those honorable formalities due to a brave warrior. Let us now give the signal for the troops to retire to rest. We will then divide the honors that we have won today.

[Exit.]

NOTES

NOTES

NOTES

NOTES

NOTES

NOTES

NOTES

NOTES

NOTES

NOTES

NOTES